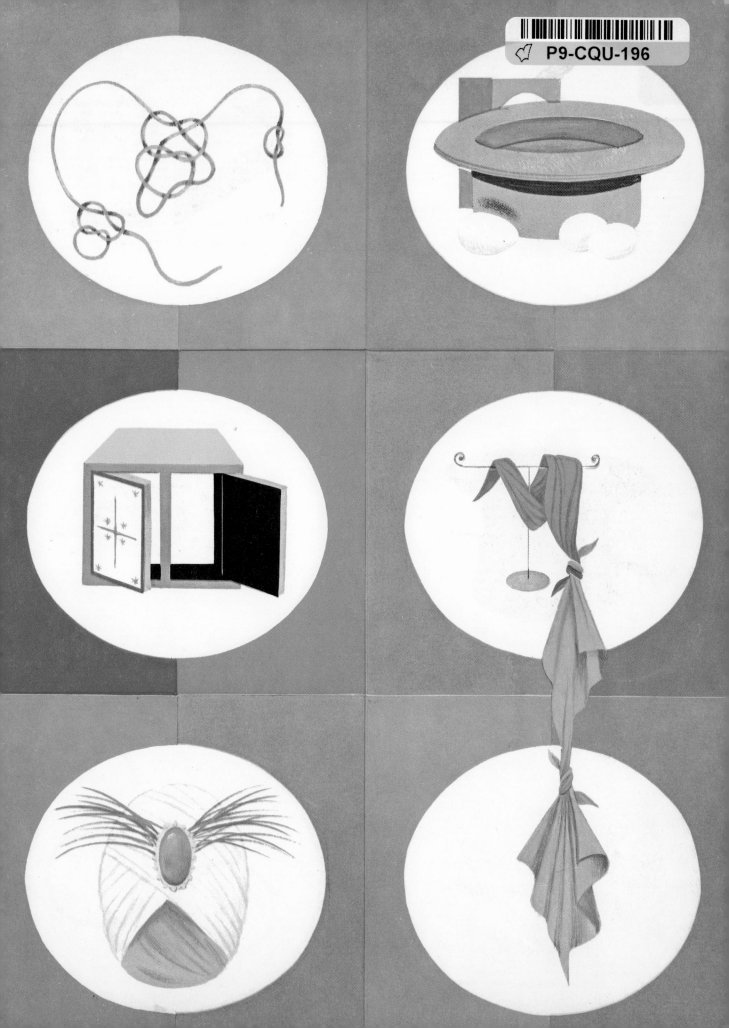

# THE GOLDEN BOOK OF
# MAGIC

## Amazing Tricks for Young Magicians

*by*

### THE GREAT MERLINI
**(Clayton Rawson)**

*Illustrated by*

### WILLIAM DUGAN

GOLDEN PRESS · NEW YORK

# Contents

Library of Congress Catalog Card Number: 64-12827

© Copyright 1964 by Golden Press, Inc. Designed and produced by Artists and Writers Press, Inc. Printed in the U.S.A. by Western Printing and Lithographing Company. Published by Golden Press, Inc., New York. Published simultaneously in Canada by The Musson Book Company, Ltd., Toronto.

# Easy Tricks
# To Begin With

## CATCH THE BILL

This is a juggling feat which looks very easy but is found to be almost impossible. Hold a fairly new, not too wrinkled, dollar bill at one end. Let it hang down vertically. Place your left thumb and forefinger on opposite sides of the center of the bill, close to it but not touching it.

Let the bill fall and catch it with your left fingers. *"This,"* you say to your audience, *"is so difficult that I had to practice eight hours a day for a year."*

No one will believe you, but when you hold the bill and they try to catch it, they all fail. If you drop the bill without warning, it slips between the fingers before they can receive orders from the brain to grab it. You can pretend to give warning by calling, *"Ready. Get set. Go!"* and drop the bill a split second before saying, *"Go!"* Or you can wait until the catcher grabs the bill, tell him he jumped the gun, and then drop it just as he opens his fingers.

You can even allow him to hold his fingers near the bottom of the bill instead of at the center. He will still miss it if you drop it unexpectedly.

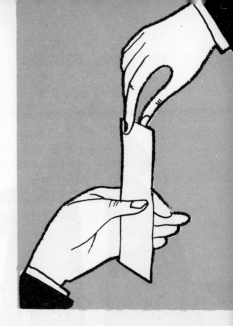

**MATERIALS**
Dollar bill

## THE LINKING CLIPS

**MATERIALS**
Dollar bill or strip of paper
10 or 12 paper clips

① Fold a dollar bill or a strip of paper so that its top edge has the shape of the letter S. Put two paper clips on the top edge as shown here.

*"Everything,"* you say, *"is being done automatically these days. This is an automatic paper-clip linker."*

Pull the ends of the bill apart quickly. The clips will fly off and link themselves together.

② Make two chains of paper clips. Put the clip at the end of each chain on the bill and have someone hold the other ends. When the bill is pulled apart the two chains will join into one.

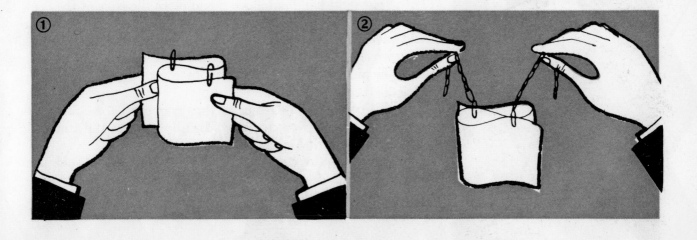

## THE SOFT PENCIL

Hold a long pencil at one end and rub its center back and forth on your coat sleeve. *"Friction,"* you say, *"creates heat, and heat makes solid objects soft and pliable."*

Then hold the pencil tightly between thumb and forefinger a little to the right of center and move your hand rapidly up and down about an inch in both directions.

Shake your head. *"No, it's not hot enough yet."* Rub it on your arm again for a moment.

Hold it near the center again, but this time hold it loosely so that when your hand moves up and down the pencil wobbles.

The pencil will appear to bend as though made of rubber. The illusion is due to the fact that the ends of the pencil travel through a greater distance than the center, which seems to move very little.

*"As it cools off, of course, it becomes rigid again."* Tighten your grip on the pencil gradually. The bending of the pencil diminishes, then stops.

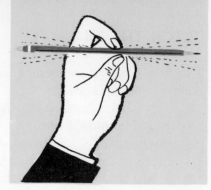

**MATERIALS**
1 pencil

## COIN BALANCE

**MATERIALS**
Half dollar
Straight pin

The performer balances a half dollar on its edge at the tips of his fingers. Then he commands it to lie down and it slowly does so.

Beforehand, obtain a common straight pin and hold it concealed between your right thumb and forefinger. Its head should be toward the tip of your finger, and your thumb should cover about half of it.

Begin by showing a half dollar (preferably borrowed from someone in the audience). Hold it in your left hand. Transfer the coin to your right hand, pushing it in under the pin. ①

*"I am going to attempt one of the most difficult of all juggling feats—watch,"* you say.

Turn your right hand palm down and place the edge of the coin on the tips of the left first and second fingers. Your left hand should have the palm up. Push the pin down between the two left fingers, which grasp and hold it tightly. Let the coin lean back ② against the pin and then, very slowly, take your right hand away, leaving the coin upright.

Hold this position for a moment, then command the coin to lie down. Loosen your grip on the pin slightly and let the coin fall slowly inward until it lies flat on your fingers.

As you pick up the coin with your right hand, turn your left hand inward so that the pin is not seen. Give the coin to someone and ask if he would like to try balancing it. At the same time, lower your left hand to your side and let the pin fall to the floor.

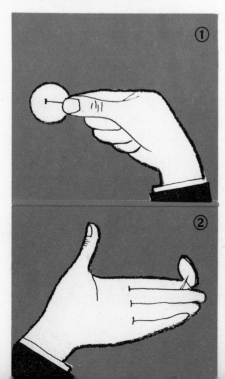

## BORROWED HANDKERCHIEF PENETRATION

The performer borrows a pocket handkerchief and pushes a pencil, a table knife, or his wand through its center, apologizes for making a hole in the handkerchief, and then mends it by magic.

Borrow a man's handkerchief, make a fist with your left hand, and cover it with the handkerchief. Your fist should be under the center of the handkerchief. Turn your left side toward your audience. ① Push the center of the handkerchief down into your fist with your right forefinger.

② Open your fist slightly, and push the right middle finger into it from the side, carrying a fold of the cloth with it.

Take both fingers out at the top. This leaves a circular tunnel in the handkerchief in the center of your fist.

③ Push a long pencil, a table knife, or your wand down into this opening. Push it in three or four inches, and move it up and down a few times, as though it were hitting the center of the handkerchief. Suddenly, push it in out of sight, then loosen your left fist and let it fall through.

*"I'm sorry,"* you say. *"I didn't mean to poke a hole through your handkerchief. I hope you don't mind."* Look down into the hole. *"That's going to be hard to fix. But I'll try."* Snap your fingers, grasp one corner with your right hand, pull the handkerchief quickly away from the left hand, spread it out and show that the hole has vanished.

**MATERIALS**
Handkerchief
Long pencil or
table knife or wand

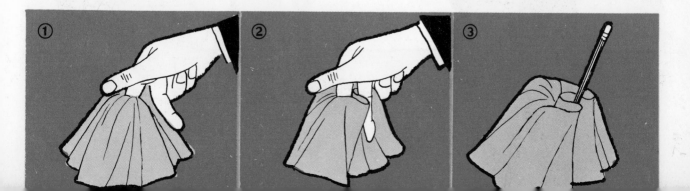

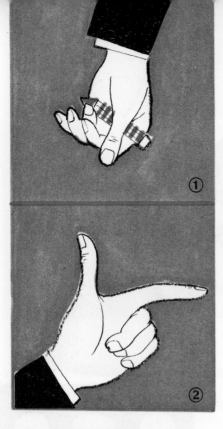

## COLOR TOUCH

Among the most mysterious of all magic tricks are those in which the magician appears to exhibit extraordinary sensory or mental powers. Here is one in which he seems to be able to see colors with his fingertips.

Give a spectator a box of wax coloring crayons. Say, *"Believe it or not, my sense of touch is so highly developed that I can see color with my fingertips."* Turn your back to your audience, put your hands behind you, and add, *"Let's try it. Give me one of the crayons."*

When you have the crayon, face your audience again. Behind ① your back, dig the fingernail of your left middle finger into the end of the crayon and get a small piece of it under your fingernail.

Then say, *"This takes a lot of concentration."* Half close the third, fourth and fifth fingers, so that the audience cannot see the fingernail. Bring your left hand around in front of you and place ② your forefinger and thumb against your forehead. As your hand moves up past your eyes get a quick look at the particle of crayon under your fingernail. Immediately close your eyes and pretend to concentrate. After a moment, name the color.

Bring your right hand forward with the crayon to show that you have named it correctly. Put your hands behind your back again, dislodge the hidden particle of crayon and you are all set to do the trick again.

If you repeat the trick too many times someone may get suspicious of the right hand, so stop after the third time and then do the "Color Divination" trick (page 92). This will throw everyone off the track because it uses a quite different method.

**MATERIALS**
Box of wax
coloring crayons

## TRICKY GLASSES

① Place three empty glasses in a row, the middle glass mouth up, the other two bottoms up.

*"Here,"* you say, *"is a curious puzzle that is harder to do after you have seen it done than before. The problem is to turn the glasses over two at a time and have them all right side up at the finish. After years of study I have found out how to do it in only three moves. Watch!"*

② Quickly take the two glasses at the left (A and B), one in each hand, and turn them over.

③ Then cross your arms, to make your movements confusing and harder to remember, and turn over the two glasses at each end (A and C).

④ Finally, turn over the two on the left (A and B) once more. Do all this quickly so that it is hard to follow.

⑤ Now turn the middle glass bottom up and ask a spectator to try the trick. *"It should be easy,"* you say. *"You just saw me do it."* Actually it is now impossible in any number of moves because the starting position (only one glass upside down instead of two) is different. If anyone does manage to duplicate your moves, all the glasses will be upside down at the finish.

If any spectator who tries it accidentally resets the glasses in the correct starting position, simply interrupt and give another quick demonstration. By doing this, you can leave the glasses in the wrong starting position.

If you continue too long someone will finally notice the difference in starting positions and catch on. A good way to finish the stunt before that happens is to announce that you can also solve the problem in *two* moves. Set the glasses in the correct starting position and quickly turn over the two glasses on the left (A and B) and then the two on the right (B and C).

Immediately go back to the starting position and add, *"I have heard that someone once figured out how to do it in one move, but he kept it a secret and never told anyone."* As you say this turn the two end glasses (A and C) right side up.

Nearly everyone will have caught on by now. If there is someone who hasn't, give him the wrong starting position again and let him try to do it in any number of moves.

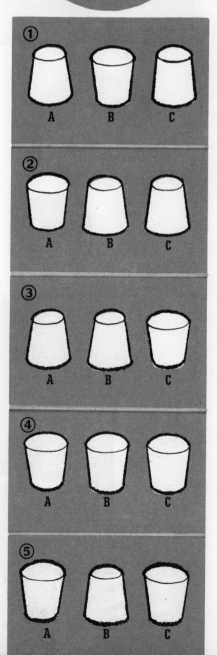

MATERIALS
3 glasses

**MATERIALS**
Bowl of cubed sugar
Glass of water
Soft lead pencil

## THE MYSTIC MARK

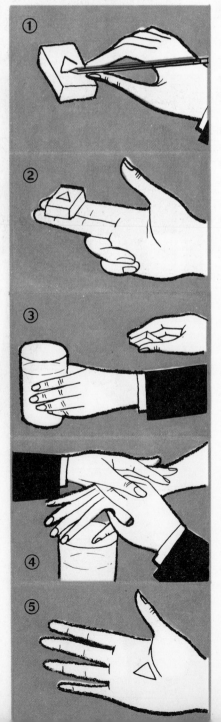

Hindu fakirs perform a mystifying feat in which a spectator draws something on a pebble which is then thrown into the sacred river Ganges. Then the spectator holds his hand out toward the river while the magician mutters magic incantations. A moment later the spectator finds that his drawing has magically returned from the river and is now on his hand.

You can do this with a cube of sugar and a glass of water. Ask someone to select a cube of sugar from a bowl. Have him remove the paper wrapper if there is one. Then give him a soft pencil and ask him to draw a letter of the alphabet or some simple design ① on one side of the cube.

While the spectator is doing this, take a drink from your glass of water and let a few drops of water run over onto the outside edge of the glass. As you put the glass down, dampen the ball of your thumb by running it across the wet spot.

Take the sugar cube from the spectator with your right hand ② and show the mark to your audience. Now, if you press your dampened thumb against the mark it will leave an impression on your thumb. But you must do this without its being seen. Bring your right hand in toward your body and at the same time push the water glass out to the center of the table with your left hand. The spectators will look at the glass, and as they do, place your ③ thumb on the mark and turn the right hand over, palm down, at the same time.

Immediately upon doing this, move your right hand forward to the glass and drop the sugar into the water, turning it so that it falls with the mark up.

Then ask the spectator to cover the mouth of the glass with his hand. No matter how he does this, tell him it isn't quite right.

Take his hand off the glass with both of yours, pressing your ④ right thumb lightly against his palm—and keep talking. *"You must keep all your fingers perfectly straight."* Then put his hand back on the mouth of the glass.

This action has transferred an impression of the mark to his hand. Now call the spectator's attention to the fact that the mark on the sugar is slowly disappearing, which it does as the sugar dissolves. Wait until the mark is completely gone, then tell the spectator to turn his hand over.

The mark that vanished in the water has mysteriously drifted ⑤ up and appeared on his hand!

## BEHIND YOUR BACK

Announce that you are going to prove that you have eyes in the back of your head. Turn your back and tell someone in your audience to make up three piles of matches (or any other small objects: toothpicks, sugar cubes, coins, playing cards).

*"You may use as many matches as you like, but put the same number in each pile, and put more than three in each pile to make it difficult."*

When you are told this has been done, say, *"Now take three matches from each of the end piles and put them in the center pile."*

When this has been done you continue, *"Count the number in either of the end piles, take that number away from the center pile, and put those taken away in either of the end piles."*

No matter how many matches are being used, this always leaves nine matches in the center pile. But since some people know about the magical properties of the number nine, don't stop here. Ask that several more matches be either added or subtracted from the center pile. When you have been told how many have been added or removed, make the addition or subtraction mentally. For example, if four more matches have been taken away from the center pile, there are five left.

*"Since I have eyes in the back of my head, I see that there are five matches remaining in the center pile. Will you please count them and confirm that."*

Someone in your audience may suspect that the answer is always the same, so you disprove this by doing the trick again and getting a different answer.

Another way to present this is to ask the spectator, after he has formed the three piles, to name any number between one and twelve. Then give instructions that will leave the chosen number of matches in the center pile. When he discovers what has happened, tell him, *"You seem to be able to predict ahead of time what will happen. You should go into business as a fortune teller!"*

**MATERIALS**
Matches or other
small objects

## THE SECRET NUMBER

A spectator thinks of a number, remembers the name of the card that lies at that number in a group of cards, and the performer finds it almost at once without asking any questions.

Give someone from your audience ten cards and ask him to shuffle them. As he does this, say, *"Think of any number from one to ten and keep it a deep dark secret. Spread the cards you hold out so you can see all their faces. Then count from the right to*  *your secret number, and remember the card in that position."*

After this has been done, take the cards from the spectator, spread them and glance at their faces. Take off the top five cards and put them behind the others.

Give the cards back to the spectator. *"Since I saw the cards, let's change the position of your card. Hold the cards face up, count down to your secret number again, and put the counted cards under the others. I'll look the other way while you do that.*

*"Now spread the cards out again so you can see the faces of all of them, but don't let me see them. If I only knew your secret number, I could find your card. But don't tell me. I am going to try to find it without any clue at all."*

Reach out, run your finger over the backs of the cards he holds,  count from *your left* over to the fifth card, and pull it up out of the fan of cards.

*"You're thinking of this one!"*

Just follow these instructions. It will always be the fifth card.

The performer shows a spectator how to find his own chosen card magically. This card trick can be done with several spectators simultaneously.

If you have learned "The Secret Number" trick above, you already know how to do this one. The same method is used, but it is presented differently and has a different climax.

Begin by asking, *"Would you like to do a trick yourself?"* Then give ten cards to each person who wants to try it, and give the same instructions as in "The Secret Number" trick. After everyone has chosen his own secret number and looked at the card which lies at that number in his packet, go to each person in turn. Take each packet of ten cards, glance at the faces, and this time move *three* cards from the face to the back of the packet.

Then, after everyone has transferred his secret number of cards from the face to the back of the packet he holds, proceed as follows.

## YOU FIND IT

*"Hold your cards face down. Deal off one card, then put the*  *next card underneath all the others. Deal another card and put*  *the next card underneath. Continue doing this until you have only one card left."*

When this has been done, ask each person in turn to name his card aloud, then turn up the one he holds. They will all discover that they have found their own cards!

① 

② 

① 

② 

## THE RADIO MIND

The performer turns his back while a spectator selects a card and then buries it in the deck. The spectator is asked to broadcast the name of his card by sending out thought waves. The performer deals the cards, apparently picks up the mental broadcast, and stops at the correct card.

Begin by having a spectator shuffle a deck of cards.

Take the shuffled deck and say, "*After I turn my back, you are to deal cards off the top into a pile one at a time. Like this.*" Deal several cards, but count them mentally and remember the number. (For example, let's say you deal six.)

"*You may stop whenever you like. Then look at the last card dealt, remember it, and drop the rest of the deck on it.*" Demonstrate this by lifting the last card you just dealt, glimpse its face, remember it, and then place the remainder of the deck on top of it.

Give the deck to the spectator and turn your back. Remind the spectator to deal silently so that you can't hear how many cards he deals. And repeat your instructions to make sure that he follows them correctly. "*Deal as many cards as you like, look at the last one dealt, and drop the deck on top.*" When he says he has done this, tell him to cut the deck, so that his chosen card will be buried in the middle of the deck.

Take the deck and say, "*I have a radio mind and if you will broadcast the name of your card mentally, I'll try to tune in on your program.*"

Begin dealing the cards one at a time, face up, and watch for the card you glimpsed. When it turns up, stop, and say, "*Your thought waves are coming in fine, but now you're broadcasting a commercial. Do you have to do that? Please think only of your card.*"

You now know exactly how far down in the remainder of the deck the chosen card is. (If you dealt six cards when you were showing the spectator how to deal, it is now sixth from the top.) Now close your eyes, pretend to concentrate deeply, and don't look at the rest of the cards as you deal. Deal them one at a time, hold each one up so the spectators can see it, then drop it face down. When you reach the chosen card, stop, and say, "*You're thinking of this one.*"

MATERIALS
Deck of playing cards

## MENTAL BROADCAST

A spectator chooses a card while the performer's back is turned, and places it with some other cards in his pocket. The magician reaches into the pocket, and brings out one card which proves to be the chosen one.

Give someone about one-third of the deck, and ask him to shuffle the cards thoroughly. Turn your back while he does this.

Then tell him, *"When you have finished shuffling, look at the bottom card and remember it. Next, think of a number between one and fifteen. Count that number of cards off the top of the deck and put them on the bottom."*

① Take the cards from the spectator. *"Please concentrate on your card. I'll try to stop dealing when I come to it, without ever seeing the faces of any of the cards."*

Deal cards off the deck into a face-down pile. Be sure to deal the cards one at a time, because this reverses their order and that is important.

Stop dealing for a moment about halfway through and ask, *"Are you sure you are concentrating? I don't seem to be getting any thought waves."* Then deal the rest of the cards. Shake your head, disappointedly. *"Nothing came through at all. Your sending apparatus must be out of order. We'll have to try something else."*

Give the cards to the spectator. *"If I could get the number you thought of, that would help. Deal off the same number of cards as before, then put them underneath the others. I won't watch you."*

Turn your back as he does this. Then face him again. *"I still didn't get anything. Your broadcasting equipment needs a complete checkup and probably some new parts. We'll have to try something else. Please put the cards in your pocket."*

The chosen card is now the top card of the packet the spectator holds. He will almost always put the cards in his pocket with this top one on the outside away from his body, but watch him and note how he does it.

Then go to the spectator, ask him to try broadcasting just once more. *"Think hard, now. That's better."*

② Reach into his pocket; riffle the cards a bit as though you were hunting through the packet. Bring out the top card. Ask the spectator to name his card, then show that you have found it.

**MATERIALS**
**Deck of playing cards**

① ②

# Match Magic

## THE FLYING MATCHES

The performer asks a spectator to solve three very easy subtraction problems, and the spectator's answers are all wrong.

PREPARATION: Put six paper matches in your right coat pocket and a quarter in the small inner change pocket.

PERFORMANCE: Ask a spectator if he can do simple subtraction and then ask him to prove it. "*Here's a test.*"
  Open a match folder, tear out two matches and lay them down.
  Tip the folder up so that its flap hides the remaining matches ① and apparently tear out a third match, but actually take two.
  Drop one of the matches with the first two and close your ② fingers around the other match, concealing it from your audience.

**MATERIALS**
2 match folders
1 quarter

Pick up one match with your right forefinger and thumb, count *"One,"* and place it on the palm of your left hand.

③ Pick up a second match and count, *"Two."*

④ As you put the second match in your left hand, start to close the left fingers. Open the right fingers so that the concealed match is also added to the two already in the left hand.

⑤ Pick up the last match and put it in your right pocket as you count *"Three."*

While your hand is still in your pocket, say, *"Here's the first problem. One match from three leaves how many?"*

When the spectator answers, *"Two,"* say, *"You're going to have to stay after school and write on the blackboard five hundred times: one from three equals three."* Turn your left hand over and drop the three matches it holds.

As you do this, bring your right hand out of your pocket with one match concealed in it.

*"I'll give you a second chance."* Pick up one of the matches and put it in your left hand. This time let the concealed match fall with the first match. Pick up a second match and place it in your left hand. Without drawing attention to the fact, let the audience see that your right hand is empty.

Place the third match in your right pocket, gather up the six extra matches and conceal them under your curled fingers.

*"How much is one from three?"* If the spectator still answers, *"Two,"* say, *"You don't learn very quickly, do you?* If he answers *"Three"* this time, say, *"That's much better; now you've learned something."* Again throw out the three matches.

Then say, *"Here's a harder problem. This time I'll only put one match in my hand."* Pick up one match. Drop it into your left hand together with the seven others you have taken out of your pocket.

*"And I'll put two in my pocket. How much is two from three?"* Pick up two matches, put them in your pocket, leave them there, and get the quarter, holding it concealed under your curled fingers as before.

The spectator may reply *"One,"* or he may say *"Three."* He's wrong either way. Throw out all the matches as you say, *"Two from three leaves eight! Anybody knows that."*

Bring your right hand from your pocket, pick up one of the matches, and tear it in half. *"I guess these problems are too hard for you. Here's a very easy one. This time I'll put half a match in my hand, and all the others in my pocket."*

As you say this, pretend to put the half match in your hand, but let the quarter fall in instead. Immediately reach out with your right hand (the half match is so small it is easily hidden between your thumb and forefinger). Scoop up all the remaining matches. Place them in your pocket and leave them there.

*"Seven and one-half from eight leaves how much?"* Then, no matter what the spectator replies, say, *"It usually leaves a half—except on Tuesdays"* (or whatever the day happens to be when you perform this trick)—*"and then it only leaves a quarter."* Open your hand showing the quarter.

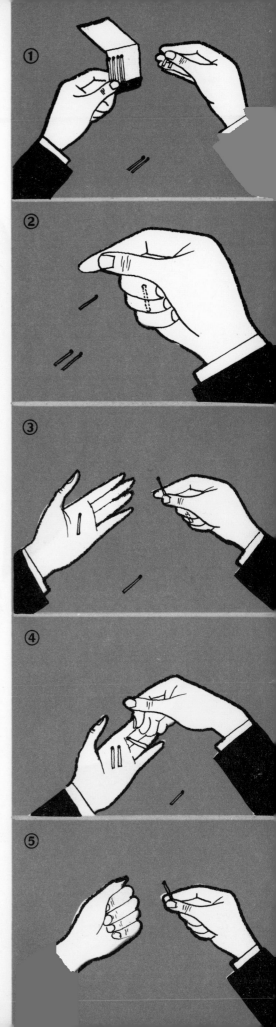

## COLOR-CHANGING MATCHES

A paper match changes color instantly and visibly several times.

Most paper matches are a dark color on one side and a lighter color on the other. Hold such a match at one end between thumb ① and forefinger as shown.

Turn your hand over to the left so that it is back up. During the ② turn, twist the match with your fingers, giving it a half turn. If this is done while the hand and match are in motion the half turn cannot be seen even when it is done slowly.

The spectators have apparently seen that both sides of the match are the same color. Turn your hand palm up again, twisting the match in the opposite direction. If the match tends to slide rather than turn, moisten your fingers slightly, or hold the match by the head, which is rounded and easier to twist.

Now shake the match by moving your hand very quickly three or four inches to the right, then back again. Twist the match as you do so and it appears to change color visibly. Turn your hand over, not too fast, twist the match again, and apparently show that the opposite side has also changed color.

Another way to present this is to show that the light-colored match turns dark when it touches a dark object, and then becomes light again when it touches a light-colored object. The match is given a half twist as you reach out to touch something with it. Always make the twist while your hand is moving so that it cannot be seen.

A little advance preparation will enable you to give the match to a spectator so that he can examine it and see that both sides really are the same color. Make a match which is the same on both sides by splitting two matches and rubber-cementing two like-colored halves together. Put this match back in the folder, wedging it under the striking surface at the left side. When you open the folder as you begin, put your thumb directly on this prepared match and slide it to the left onto the fingers of your left hand. Then tear out another match with your right hand, close the folder and replace it in your pocket. Curl your left fingers, except for your index finger, over the prepared match, hiding it.

Now, after the second match has changed color a few times, ③ take it between your left thumb and index finger by its head.

Extend your left hand toward a spectator, turn it palm down, and open the other fingers. This hides the color-changing match and releases the prepared one at the same time.

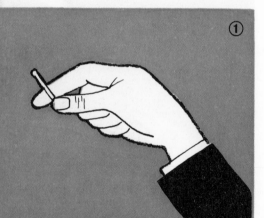

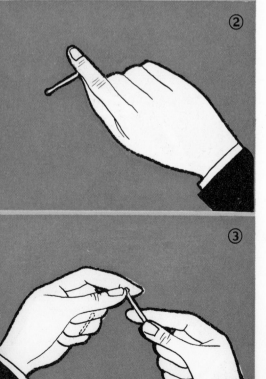

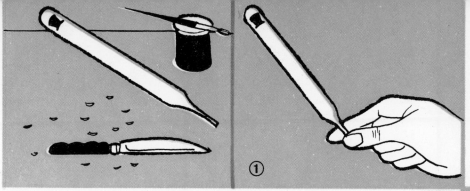

①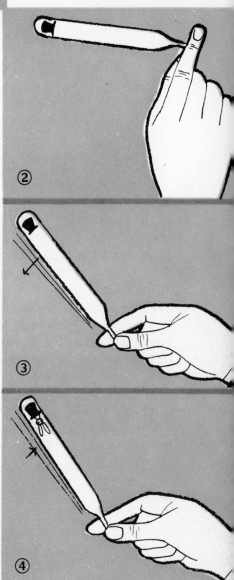

## THE RABBITS IN THE HATS

The performer shows a small paddle which bears the picture of a top hat on both sides. Suddenly a rabbit appears in one hat, then a second rabbit in the other hat, and then finally both rabbits disappear.

PREPARATION: Once you have learned to do "Color-Changing Matches" trick, you can also do this one because the method is the same.

Get a wooden tongue depressor from your drug store. Whittle it at one end into the shape shown here. Paint it some bright color; the unpainted wood will become dirty from use and the paint will prevent this.

Trace the drawings of the hat and the rabbit in the hat on white tracing paper and ink them in. Cut both drawings out and paste them on opposite sides of the paddle. Make sure that the distance from the bottom of the hat to the end of the paddle is the same on both sides.

① PERFORMANCE: Hold the paddle between thumb and index finger at the narrow end and show the hat drawing. Turn your hand over
② and twist the paddle, giving it a half turn as explained under "Color-Changing Matches," thus showing a hat on both sides.

*"This hat, like all magicians' hats, contains a rabbit. Would you like to see him?"*

③ Jerk the paddle quickly five or six inches to the left and then back again, twisting it at the same time. A rabbit appears
④ instantly.

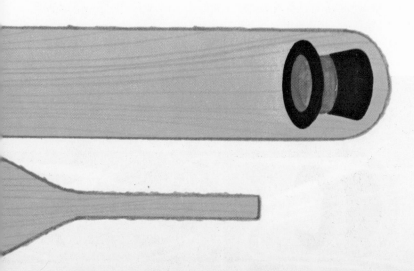

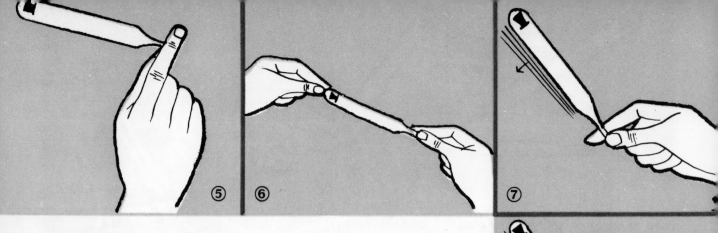

(5)    ⑤    ⑥

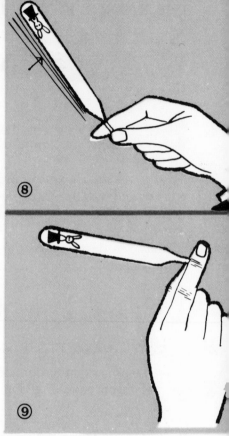

⑤    Turn your hand over to the left *without* twisting the paddle, and show that the second hat is still empty. Take the upper end

⑥ of the paddle with your left hand, remove your right hand for a moment, turn it palm up and then take hold of the paddle again.

⑦⑧    Shake the paddle, causing a second rabbit to appear. Turn the

⑨ paddle over, twisting it again, and show that there are rabbits in both hats.

Place your left hand palm down over the paddle, covering it, and say, "*Go!*" Twist the paddle at the same time, remove the left hand, and show that the rabbit has vanished.

Turn the paddle over showing the rabbit in the other hat; ask a spectator to cover it with his hand and say "*Go!*" Another twist and this rabbit also disappears. Show both sides of the paddle once more, showing both hats empty as at the beginning.

When people find that you can do magic, one of the first questions they ask is: "*Can you take a rabbit from a hat?*" With this paddle handy you are ready to do it at any time.

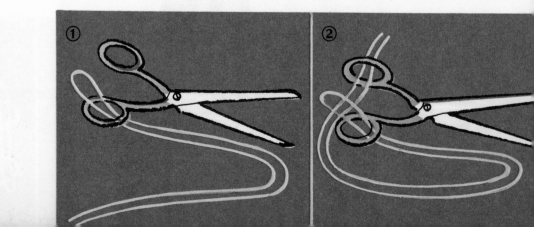

# String Sorcery

## THE MAGIC SCISSORS

A pair of scissors, threaded on a string, is magically released.

①    Hold a long piece of string (about six feet) at its center and push the center through one of the handles of a pair of scissors.

②    Then put both ends of the string through this center loop and through the other handle.

Ask a spectator to hold the ends of the string. Turn your back, hiding the scissors from view.

*"I could get the scissors off the string by cutting it, but magicians always do things the hard way."*

③    Pull the center loop (A) out several inches, and put it through
④  handle (B). Then, being careful not to twist the loop, open it
⑤  out, pass it completely over the scissors, and tell the spectator to pull on the ends. The string comes free from the scissors. The faster you do this the more impossible it seems.

**MATERIALS**
Scissors
6 feet of string

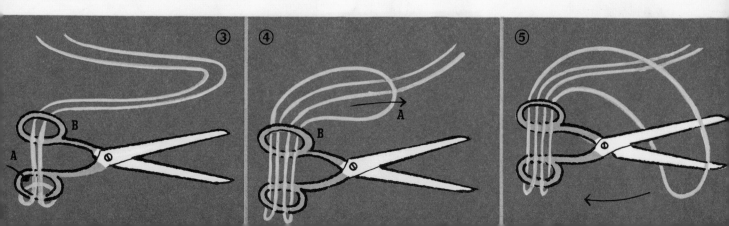

In the next two tricks a match box cover and several Lifesavers®
are magically removed from a string whose ends are held. Done in
sequence with "The Magic Scissors," they make a baffling routine.
Remove the scissors first, then the match cover, then the Lifesavers. Each trick appears to be more difficult than the preceding one.

## MATCH BOX PENETRATION

The cover of a box of safety matches is threaded on a string. Both
ends are securely held by spectators, and the magician apparently
makes the cover pass through the string.

PREPARATION: Wooden match box covers have one side which is
made of a double thickness of wood. Insert the corner of a razor  ①
blade between the two strips and slit the paper that holds them
together.

Apply a coat of rubber cement to these overlapping sides, let  ②
it dry; then apply a second coat. Fold the cover together again
with one cemented surface on the inside of the box, the other on  ③
the outside. Replace the drawer.

PERFORMANCE: Show the match box, keeping the cemented side
toward yourself so that it is not seen. Remove the drawer, then
push one end of a four-foot length of string through the cover.
Have the ends of the string held by two spectators.  ④

*"The miracle you are about to see,"* you say, *"is accomplished
with the aid of spirits. Since they work only in the dark, I'll cover
the match box with a handkerchief."*

Put both hands under the handkerchief, open the cover, and lift  ⑤
out the string. Put the cover back together again so that the cemented surfaces join, and press them firmly together.

Pronounce the magic words, *"Abracadabra hocus pocus."* Then
remove the handkerchief and toss the match cover to a spectator.
Both cover and string can be examined without revealing any
clue to the mystery.

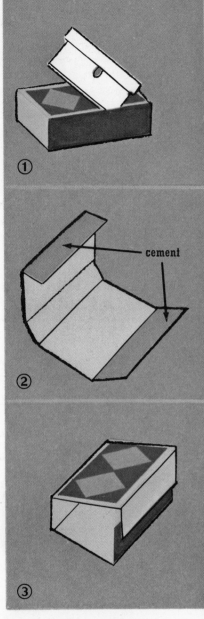

① 

cement

② 

③ 

**MATERIALS**
Match box
4 feet of string
Single edge razor blade
(Handle carefully!)
Rubber cement
Handkerchief

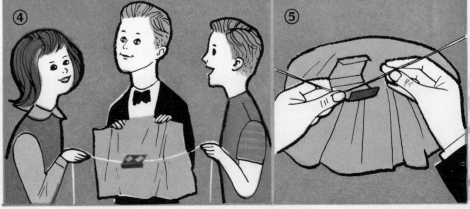

④ 

⑤

# THE GREAT CHINESE ROBBERY I

Several Chinese coins (or Lifesaver® candy mints, which are easier to obtain) are threaded onto a string. The ends of the string are held by a spectator, and the magician, playing the part of a Chinese pickpocket, steals the money by removing it magically from the center of the string.

There are two methods. The first needs no preparation and can be done impromptu at any time.

PERFORMANCE: *"The Chinese have invented many things, but for centuries their clothing contained no pockets in which to carry loose change. They solved this by putting holes in their coins and carrying them on a piece of string. I spent all my Chinese money on my last trip to the Far East, so I'll use these Lifesavers."*

① Double the string and push its center through a Lifesaver, then put both ends through the loops. *"One coin is tied securely on the string."*

② *"Other coins are put on top of it."* Thread both ends of the string through several more of the Lifesavers.

Have a spectator hold the ends of the string. *"You are a wealthy Chinese banker and I am a pickpocket who wants to steal your money."*

③ Cover the Lifesavers with a handkerchief. Then pull down on loop (A) until it is large enough to slip over the bottom Lifesaver.

Take all the Lifesavers off the string and then replace one of them by pushing the string through the hole and up around the candy.

Bring the other Lifesavers out from under the handkerchief one at a time and give them to the spectators.

Lift the handkerchief away, showing that one Lifesaver is still tied on the string. *"Stretching those coins so they pass over the bottom one isn't easy, but the hard part is still to come. A skillful pickpocket can even get the last one."*

Cover the remaining Lifesaver with the handkerchief, remove it as before, and let the spectators examine everything.

*"No one,"* you finish, *"has ever discovered how the Chinese pickpockets do this."*

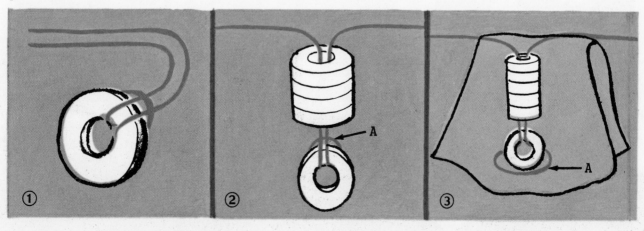

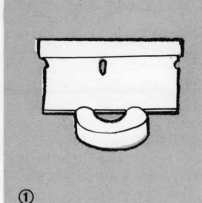

## THE GREAT CHINESE ROBBERY II

This is another way to do the same trick. A little secret preparation makes it even more baffling.

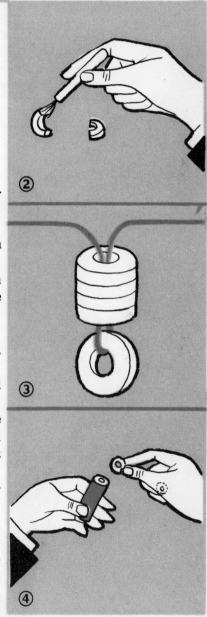

① PREPARATION: Cut a Lifesaver® in half by pressing down firmly on it with a sharp knife or razor blade.

② Apply a coating of rubber cement to the cut ends, let it dry, then put the Lifesaver back together. The join will be invisible. Replace this Lifesaver in the package on top of the others.

PERFORMANCE: The prepared Lifesaver goes on the string first and, this time, only *one* end of the string is threaded through it.

③ Ask someone to thread both ends of the string through several more Lifesavers.

④ As you take the mints from the package and give them to the spectator one at a time, secretly steal one and hold it concealed under the closed second, third, and fourth fingers of the right hand.

Under cover of the handkerchief, break the cemented Lifesaver apart, and hide the pieces in the same way in the left hand.

Then bring out your right hand and show the hidden Lifesaver. "*All I have to do,*" you say, "*is remove the bottom coin, and others naturally fall off.*" Let the remaining Lifesavers drop, then remove the broken halves in your pocket. The exchange of the extra mint for the broken one leaves you with the same number you had at the beginning in case anyone counts them.

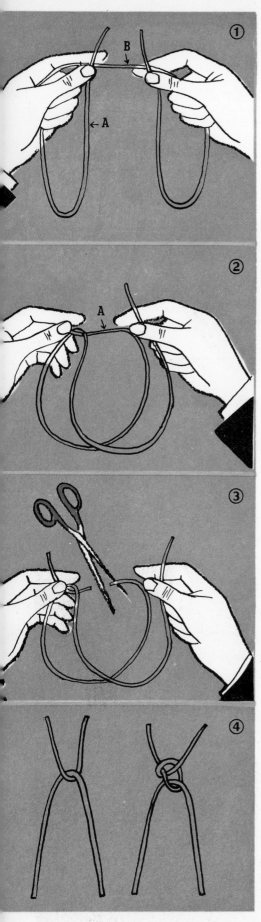

## CUT AND RESTORED STRING

A length of string is cut in half by a spectator and the performer restores it into one piece.

This trick is hundreds of years old and as good today as it ever was. One method of performing it was described in Reginald Scott's *Discoverie of Witchcraft*, the first book in English to explain magicians' tricks, printed in 1584.

Before you begin, put your scissors on a table to your right. Then hold a three-foot length of string between the thumb and forefinger of each hand about an inch from the ends. Lift one knee, lay the center of the string on it, and then pick up the center with the same fingers so that the string is held as shown here. ①

You now make one secret move which the spectators do not see. You cover it by misdirecting their attention away from it. Turn your body to the right, point with both hands toward the scissors, and ask someone to come forward and get them. At the *same moment*, while your audience's attention is on the scissors and the spectator, your right fingers let go of the center of the string at B and grasp it again at A instead. ②

Now, what the audience believes to be the center of the string is actually a section close to the left end.

Ask the spectator to cut the string at the center. Then ask him ③ to choose either pair of ends. If he chooses the pair in your right hand, give him one end to hold and give the other to another spectator. If he chooses the ends in your left hand, say, "*Good, I'll tie those ends together,*" and have the spectators hold the other pair of ends. It makes no difference which pair of ends are chosen, you always tie those at the left. But the fact that a choice was given makes it seem later that either pair of ends could have been restored.

When you tie together the ends of what appear to be two strings of equal length, you are really tying one very short piece ④ around the center of a long piece.

Take the scissors and say, "*I'll trim off the ends of the knot so that it looks neater.*" Cut off about half of the ends, then pull the knot up to the finger tips and cut it off, being careful not to cut the long string.

Make a magic pass over your left hand with the scissors and ask the spectators to pull on the string. When its center comes out of your hand, the two pieces have been magically joined into one!

**MATERIALS**
Scissors
3 feet of string

# Rope and Knot Magic

Some of the best tricks in magic are those done with rope or string. Rope is best because it is easier to handle and, being thicker, can be seen more easily when you are performing for a group of people. It should be white and soft and pliable. The best is a soft woven rope which can be obtained at stores which sell materials for magic tricks. Stores which sell boating supplies also have ropes and thick cords which can be used. If you use string, get the thickest white wrapping cord. If this tends to twist, give it a single turn around a chair rung and pull it back and forth to remove the kinks. Here are several quick tricks arranged in a routine so they can be done in sequence.

## SELF-TYING KNOT

Use a four-foot length of rope. Secretly tie a loose knot about six inches from one end before you begin the trick.

①     Display the rope but keep the knot hidden under the curled fingers of the right hand.

②     Pick up the lower end of the rope and place it in the right hand, holding it in the crotch of the thumb. Count *"One!"* Make a quick downward throw and drop the unknotted end. Repeat the same action at the count of *"Two!"*

③     Once more repeat what looks like the same action, count *"Three!"* but this time throw down the other end of the rope. The knot appears mysteriously, as though it had tied itself.

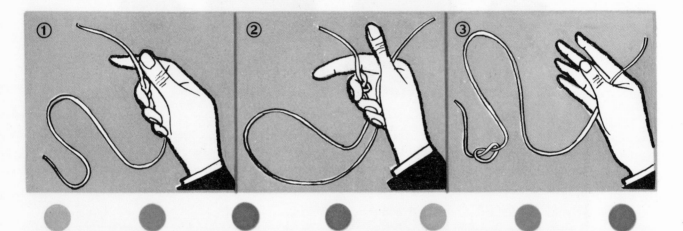

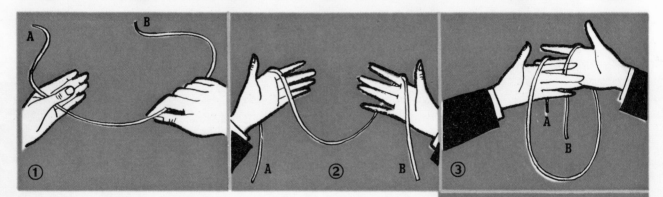

## INSTANTANEOUS KNOT

①   Hold the rope with the left hand, palm up, about six inches from end A. The right hand, palm down, holds end B as shown here.

②   Turn the right hand inward, fingers going under the rope to the position shown here.

Say, *"I am going to try to break the world's record for tying an overhand knot. Ready! Get set! Go!"* Bring your hands together quickly.

③   Your right hand goes behind the left and its first and second fingers grasp end A while the left first and second fingers grasp end B.

④   Then pull the hands apart and the knot forms in the center.

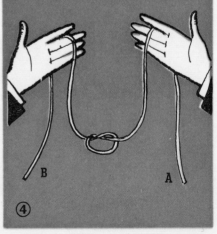

# INSTANTANEOUS KNOT WITH ONE HAND

This knot tie appears to be very difficult but is actually quite easy.
① Hold the rope as shown here so that it passes between the two middle fingers and over the thumb. End A should hang down about ten inches. All you have to do is turn your hand over in the
② direction shown by the arrow and grasp end A between thumb and forefinger. Then shake your hand so that the loop around
③ the hand falls off and there's the knot! If you practice this so you can do it fast, the spectators won't be able to follow you. It will look as though you simply gave the rope a shake and made a knot.

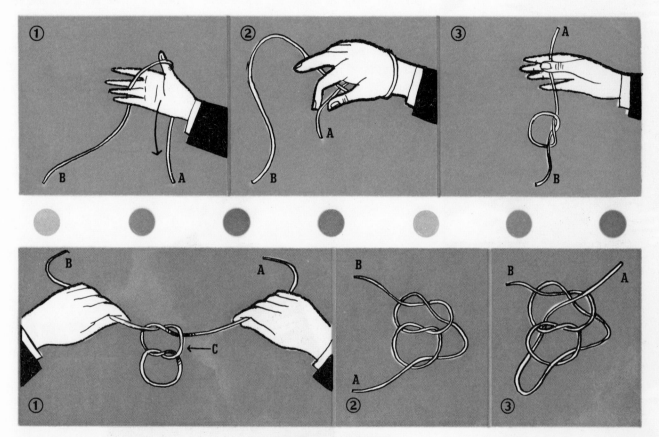

## A VANISHING KNOT

After tying either of the instantaneous knots, show that they can be untied just as mysteriously. Tell your audience, *"The easiest way to untie a knot is to tie several more."*

① The first knot, the lower one, is a half hitch. Tie a second half hitch above it. Make sure that the shaded sections of the rope are both on the same side of segment C so that the two knots together form a square knot, not a granny. Keep the loops open as shown.

② As you say, *"We tie these two knots together with a third knot,"* push end A through the lower loop from the far side.

③ Then push end A through the top loop, also from the far side. When you pull both ends of the rope apart slowly, the knots get smaller and smaller and then disappear.

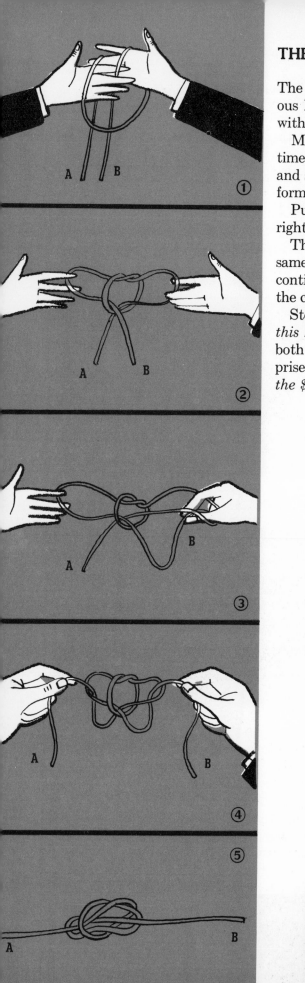

## THE VANISHING SHOELACE KNOT

The starting position here is the same as in the first "Instantaneous Knot" trick except that you hold your hands closer together with only seven or eight inches of rope between them.

Move the hands together, left hand inside the right, and this ① time instead of grasping the opposite ends of the rope with the first and second fingers grasp the rope as shown. Pull the hands apart, ② forming a shoelace knot. Pull it tight.

Push the right thumb and forefinger through the loop on the ③ right from the side nearest you. Reach down and grasp end B.

The left thumb and forefinger go through the left loop in the same way and take end A. Pull the ends through the loops and ④ continue pulling until the loops are drawn in close to the knot in the center, as shown. ⑤

Stop here and say, *"I will pay $10,000 to anyone who can untie this knot without cutting the rope."* Just as you say "rope," pull both ends. The large knot vanishes without a trace! Look surprised. *"That's funny. That never happened before. I guess I win the $10,000!"*

## THE ESCAPING PRISONER

The magician, securely tied, makes a miraculous escape.

**MATERIALS**
2 foot length of rope
10 or 12 foot length of rope

Use a two-foot length of rope and ask a spectator to tie one end around your left wrist. See that he doesn't tie it too tightly—just tight enough so that it obviously cannot slip off over your hand. If he tries to tie it too snugly, tell him, *"Not so tight, please. You're choking me."* He can tie as many knots as he likes. Then have the other end of the rope tied around your right wrist in the same way.

*"A prisoner handcuffed like this,"* you say, *"could still run away, so we'll make that impossible."* Give the spectator another length of rope ten or twelve feet long. Have him put one end over the rope between your hands, then hold both ends of the long rope securely.

*"Most prisoners, handcuffed and tied this way, would give up and go quietly along to jail. But not a magician!"*

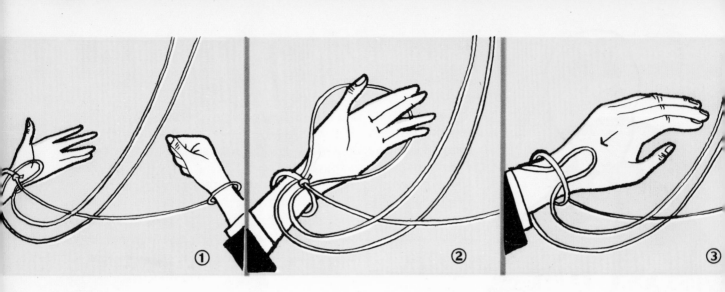

① Turn away from your audience so they cannot see what you do next. Take the center of the long rope and push it under the rope tied around the inside of your left wrist.

② Pull the long rope up and over the left hand.

③ Bring the loop down the back of the hand and again push it under the rope around your wrist.

As soon as it is completely through, the long rope drops off and the "prisoner" is free. Do this as fast as you can so that it is quite obvious that you did not have time to untie and retie any of the knots. This trick looks completely impossible and it is one of the best escape tricks that you can do.

## THE IMPOSSIBLE KNOT

When you have learned how to do the "Escaping Prisoner" trick you have actually learned three tricks because the next two are done in the same way, although they look quite different.

"I made my escape," you say, "by making one rope pass magically right through the other. Now I'll make the rope between my hands pass through itself." Turn your back again.

① Make a loop in the center of the rope and twist it three times so it looks as shown. Then push the loop in the direction of the arrow under the rope around the wrist.

Pull the loop through and slip it over your ② hand. Push the loop down along the wrist and under the rope around the wrist, just as you did in "The Escaping Prisoner." Then put the loop over your hand once more and you will find that a knot has formed on the center of the rope.

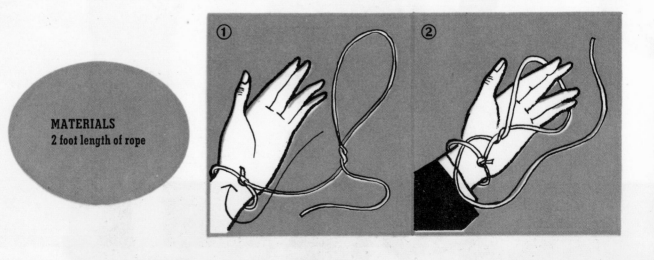

MATERIALS
2 foot length of rope

## THE RING ON THE ROPE

Follow "The Impossible Knot" with this trick. Show a rubber Mason jar ring and say, "*I shall pass this solid rubber ring through the rope. This is twice as impossible as the first two tricks.*"

Turn your back and put your left hand through the rubber ring. ①

Slide the ring up your wrist and in under the rope. ②

When it reaches this position all you have to do is take the ring ③ off the hand, this time letting it pass over the rope. ④

This puts the ring on the rope. ⑤

Finally, slide the ring along the rope and push it into the knot ⑥ as shown here. Face your audience, go forward and let them examine the ring to satisfy themselves that it is one solid piece. You can say, "*I would teach you how to do this, except that I have never been able to figure it out myself!*"

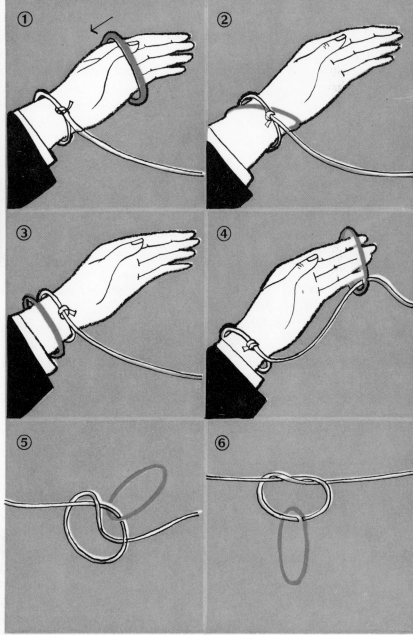

**MATERIALS**
2 foot length of rope
Rubber Mason jar ring

# Money Magic

### THE SPINNING COIN

A half dollar is placed on edge on a table and held in that position ① by the tip of your left forefinger on its top edge.

Place the tips of the right fingers on the back of the finger that holds the coin and slide them quickly forward and off the end ② of the finger. Do this several times. Suddenly, for no apparent reason the coin begins spinning. When other people try it, nothing ③ happens.

It spins for you because the last time you stroke your left forefinger your right thumb moves out unseen beneath the right hand and strikes the edge of the coin.

**MATERIALS**
Half dollar

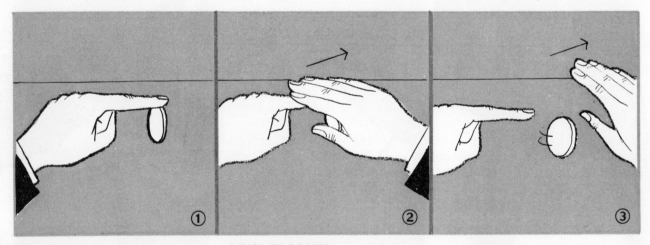

① ② ③

### COIN FLIGHT

A marked coin, covered by a handkerchief, flies invisibly through the air and into a hat on the other side of the room.

**MATERIALS**
Hat
Handkerchief
Soft pencil
2 quarters

You need a hat, a handkerchief, a soft pencil, and, in your right trouser pocket, two quarters. Begin by giving the hat to someone, asking him to make sure that it is empty. Then have him place it, brim up, across the room on a table or chair.

While he is doing this, put your right hand in your pocket, pick up one of the quarters, place it on the middle two fingers, and ① close them over it. Take the second coin between thumb and forefinger, take it out of your pocket, and show it to your audience.

Give the second coin and your pencil to a spectator and ask him to mark it for identification. When he has done this, take the pencil back with your left hand and put it in your inside breast pocket. (If you are not wearing a coat put it in your left trouser pocket.) Then take the marked coin and hold it as before between the right thumb and forefinger.

"*I am,*" you announce to your audience, "*going to make this marked coin travel magically across the room and into the empty hat. Would you like to see it go visibly or invisibly?*"

If they reply, "Visibly," which they almost always do, say, "*That's easy!*" Then go to the hat, put the marked coin into it, and leave the second coin there at the same time.

If the answer should be "Invisibly," say, "*I'll do it both ways,*" and do it visibly first.

Then say, "*But that's not magic. Let's do it the hard way—invisibly.*" Reach into the hat and bring out the unmarked coin. The absence of the mark won't be noticed because you are at some distance from the spectators.

Walk away from the hat and transfer the coin to your left hand, holding it between thumb and forefinger. Get your handkerchief, shake it out and lay it over your left hand, adjusting it ② so that the coin is at the center. Then grasp the coin through the cloth for a moment between your right thumb and forefinger.

③ Push your left thumb upward, making a small fold in the cloth behind the coin, and remove the right hand.

"*I'll give you one last look at the coin.*" Grasp the front edge of the handkerchief with your right hand, and lower your left hand ④ so that the coin points toward the floor. At the same time, lift the front edge of the handkerchief up and back onto your left arm.

This partly exposes the coin so that everyone can see that it is still there. Now let both the front and back edges of the handker-⑤ chief fall down and cover the coin. It appears to be covered, but is actually behind and outside the handkerchief.

⑥ Now put your right hand, palm up, behind the handkerchief, and move it forward, lifting the edges of the handkerchief up so they point toward the audience. At the same time, push your left second and third fingers into the fold under the coin.

Ask a spectator to hold a corner of the handkerchief. Step to-⑦ ward him and move your right hand forward, pulling the handkerchief away from your left fingers. Your left hand, which does not move at all, retains the coin.

As the spectator takes the corner of the handkerchief, put your left hand in your pocket to get the pencil and leave the coin there.

Give the pencil to the spectator. "*This looks like a pencil but it is really a magic wand. Wave it three times over the handkerchief, and say 'Go!'*"

As soon as he has done this, open your hand, letting the handkerchief fall. Then grasp it again at the bottom, jerk it quickly from the spectator's fingers, and toss it in the air.

Compliment the spectator. "*You did that like an expert.*" Ask the person who marked the coin to look in the hat, see if the coin arrived safely, and verify that his mark is on it.

# Handkerchief Tricks

You can add color to your act by performing tricks with bright silk handkerchiefs. If you make your own (with some assistance on the sewing machine from your mother) avoid getting a fabric that contains too much rayon. Use a thin Oriental silk which is springy and will expand nicely without wrinkling after it has been packed into a small space. The thirty-inch scarves obtainable at department and dollar stores can be cut down into four 15″ silks, and then hemmed. Make a very narrow hem.

If possible, buy your silks at a magic shop, because the material will be right and they stock a wide variety of sizes and colors.

## ROSE TO SILK

The best way to begin a trick using a silk handkerchief is to produce it magically. In this trick the magician takes a rose from his lapel and tosses it in the air. It unfolds and becomes a handkerchief.

① Push a corsage pin up through the lapel of your jacket from the underside just below the button hole. Take a red or white silk, and
① turn one corner back on itself two or three times. Hold this small
② bundle at the tips of the left fingers, then wind the rest of the handkerchief around it. With a little practice, the resulting coil
③ of silk makes an excellent imitation of a rose.

Push the "rose" down onto the pin in your lapel so that the pin goes through the silk and keeps it from unrolling. You are now ready to produce a silk magically at any time during your performance. Simply lift the "rose" off the pin, make a magic pass over it, and then throw it in the air. Catch it as it comes down; the rose has changed into a silk handkerchief.

**MATERIALS**
Corsage pin
Red or white silk
handkerchief

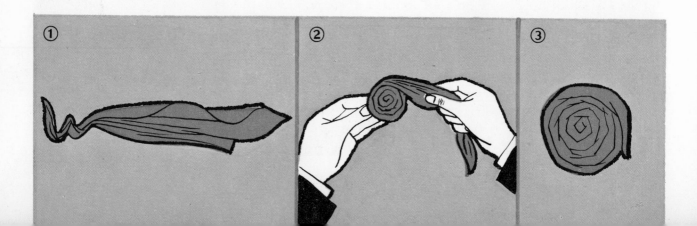

# MULTIPLYING SILKS

After the rose changes into a handkerchief, the performer sudden-ly produces two more silks of different colors from thin air.

① PREPARATION: Lay a second silk (green, perhaps) out flat, and fold two diagonally opposite corners into the center. Continue
② folding both sides in toward the center until the silk forms a band
③ about one and a half inches wide. Then fold back about two inches
④ at the left end and turn this corner up at a right angle. Beginning
⑤ at this end, roll the band tightly toward the right, and tuck the right corner into the folds at the bottom of the roll with a tooth-
⑥ pick or matchstick. The result should look like last picture below.

Roll up a third handkerchief in the same manner. Put one in your left-hand jacket pocket, along with a whistle; the other in your right-hand pocket, the projecting corners pointing forward.

**MATERIALS**
1 red or white silk handkerchief
2 silk handkerchiefs (different colors)
Toothpick or match stick
Whistle

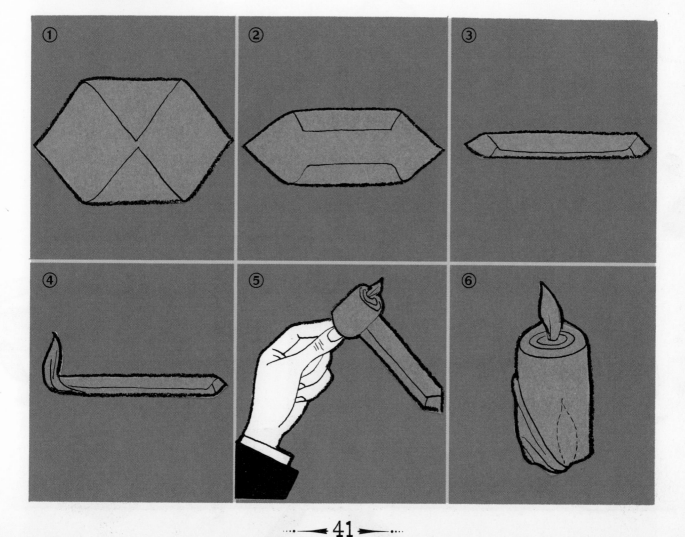

**PERFORMANCE:** After you take the rose from your lapel with your right hand (as explained in the preceding trick), place your left hand in your pocket. Take the whistle between thumb and forefinger, and curl the other fingers around the silk. Bring out both. The spectators see the whistle, but the silk is hidden under your fingers.

Put the whistle to your mouth, blow it, and throw the rose into the air. Catch the red silk as it falls with your right hand and transfer it to your left hand.

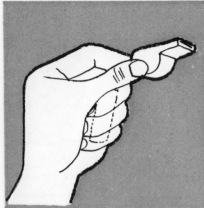

Take the whistle from your mouth with your right hand, put it in your pocket and obtain the third silk, concealing it under your curled fingers.

Bring this hand from your pocket and immediately take the red silk from your left hand as you count *"One."*

With the thumb and forefinger of your left hand, untuck the corner of the palmed silk which the left hand holds, make a downward throwing motion, and let the silk unroll as you count *"Two."*

Take the red silk with the left hand again, count *"Three,"* jerk your right hand downward, and let the third silk appear.

The change from rose to silk followed immediately by the sudden, unexpected appearance of two more silks, is really magical.

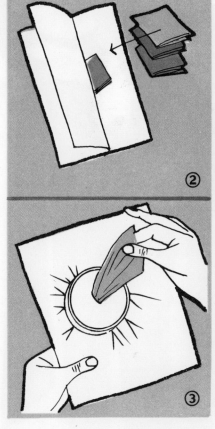

## TAMBOURINE

## PRODUCTION

The performer shows a sheet of newspaper and two embroidery hoops. He clamps the paper between the hoops, shows it on both sides, pokes a hole in the center of the paper, and pulls out two or three silks.

PREPARATION. Get two embroidery hoops at least ten inches in diameter, the larger the better.

①   Take a double page from a tabloid-size newspaper, or trim a full-size down to tabloid size (15 by 23 inches). Open it out flat. Put one of the embroidery hoops in the center of the right-hand page and draw a light pencil line around it. Apply an inch-wide coating of rubber cement around the outside of the left half of the circle. Also apply rubber cement along both sides of the center crease and extend it out toward the right about halfway on both top and bottom edges. The drawing shows the areas which the rubber cement should cover.

Then fold the left-hand page over the right-hand page. While the cement is drying, fold a silk handkerchief four times so that it makes a square one eighth the original size. Do the same with two more silks and place the three silks one on top of the other.

②   Lift the top page of the paper and insert the silks into the pocket in the center of the page.

Apply rubber cement around the right half of the circle you drew and the remaining edges of the paper. Fold the top sheet down on the cement. You now have what appears to be a single sheet of newspaper.

Hold this up to the light so you can see the position of the silks, and either remember a headline which appears in that area or draw the outline of the silks lightly with pencil on one side of the sheet.

PERFORMANCE: Show the newspaper on both sides, then place it on the smaller of the two hoops, centering the concealed pocket in the hoop. Press the large hoop down over it. Again show both sides.

Pretend to read from the paper. *"Here's an announcement of a sale of silk handkerchiefs. A magician never has to go to the store to get what he wants. I just poke a hole in the ad . . ."*

③   Poke your finger through the center of the paper and pull out the first silk, then the others.

Instead of using silks, you could put a pair of ladies' hose in the hidden pocket, then pretend to read a hosiery ad, and produce them.

MATERIALS
Silk handkerchiefs
Whistle
Sheet of newspaper
2 embroidery hoops
Rubber cement

## SILK PRODUCTION BOX

A magic box for producing silks can easily be made from cardboard. Start with a cracker or cereal box and remove the bottom completely by slitting it along the edges with a single-edge razor blade.

Then line the inside of the box with a heavier and stiffer cardboard and glue the pieces in place. Artists' illustration board, obtainable at any art supply shop, is excellent for this purpose. On another piece of the stiff cardboard draw a rectangle the same size as the inside.

Draw two triangular tabs on each side of the rectangle. If you have started with a half-pound cracker box (about 5 inches by 7½ inches), the wide ends of the triangles should measure ⅜ of an inch. If you have used a cereal box (about 7 inches by 9½ inches), this measurement can be ½ inch.

① Cut out the new shape you have drawn, as shown. Cut about halfway through the cardboard along the dotted lines so that the tabs can be bent at right angles.

② Cover the outer sides of the tabs with glue (one of the white glues is best) and glue this cardboard into the box on the side nearest the box top flap, as shown.

Then paint the inside of the box black, using a spray can. If you use a brush, paint the pieces before inserting them into the box. Finally, paint over the design on the box with a bright color.

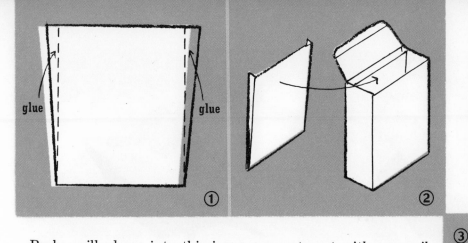

① ②

**MATERIALS**
Silk handkerchiefs
Cracker or cereal box
Single edge razor blade
(Handle carefully!)
Glue
Cardboard or
illustration board

③

④

⑤

⑥

③ Push a silk down into this inner compartment with a pencil, but let one corner project a couple of inches. Hold this corner and a corner of a second silk together and twist them around each other three or four times.

Attach each silk to the one preceding it in this way as they are tucked into the box. This is done so that as each silk is pulled out, it automatically pulls up a corner of the next one.

The smaller box mentioned will hold three 18″ silks. The larger cereal box will hold five or six. Put in as many as you can without having the sides of the box or the inner side of the secret compartment bulge. Finally, close the box top.

PERFORMANCE: Pick up the box. Open the top, folding it back as far as it will go. Hold the box like a pair of binoculars and look through it at the audience. They see into the box from the bottom and it appears to be quite empty.

The fact that the opening at the top is slightly smaller than it should be cannot be noticed. Also push your hand and arm through the box from the bottom, a further proof that it is empty.

Turn the box into a vertical position, and lift the box top up with your fingers so that it is also vertical and will hide the fact that the silks, when you produce them, come from the edge of the box.

Say, "This box looks empty, but actually there's a very small Japanese silk worm named Suki-Yaki inside who makes handkerchiefs for me to order." Look down into the box. "I need a red handkerchief—get busy." Show your hand empty and then pull out the silks, one at a time.

You can make a very amusing production out of this by not always getting what you ordered. When you order a red silk, you get a very small green one instead. Look at it disgustedly. "I wish I could speak Japanese. Suki-Yaki doesn't understand English very well." Look into the box again. "That's the wrong color and the wrong size. Try again." Then pull out a ladies' stocking, and tell Suki-Yaki, "That's not even the right shape. I want a red silk handkerchief. A square one. What?" Put your ear to the box, as if listening. "You're all out of red? Do you have blue? I'll settle for that." This time he gets it right.

If your box is large enough to hold it, a silk head scarf makes a nice final production and shows what fancy work Suki-Yaki can do when he is in the mood.

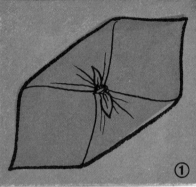

## SOLID THROUGH SOLID

Two opposite corners of a silk are tied together forming a circle, and the silk is put in a hat. A Lifesaver® is also put in the hat. A moment later the silk is removed and the candy encircles the silk.

**MATERIALS**
Silk handkerchief
Hat
Lifesaver

① PREPARATION: Thread one corner of a silk through a Lifesaver, and tie the ends together.

Roll the silk as explained under "Unlinking Silks" so that both knot and Lifesaver are hidden in the center folds.

Lay it on your table or put it in your breast pocket.

PERFORMANCE: Display the silk, holding it by one corner. Tie the ends together using the false knot (page 47).

Put the silk in a hat, and pull the false knot apart. Then show
② a Lifesaver and put it in the hat, slipping it under the sweat band.

*"Some very queer things happen in that hat. I'm beginning to think it is haunted. Look!"*

Reach into the hat, quickly find the hidden knot, and slide the
③ candy to the center of the handkerchief. Then bring it out with the right hand and at the same time lift the hat with the left hand, showing it to be empty. Toss the silk and the Lifesaver to a spectator for examination.

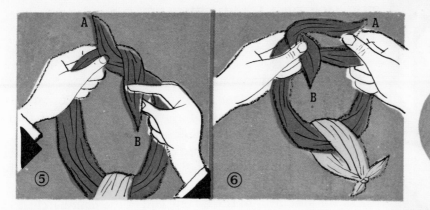

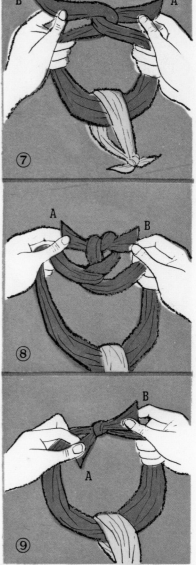

## UNLINKING SILKS

Two diagonally opposite corners of a silk are tied together forming a circle. A second silk is threaded through the circle and also tied. The linked silks mysteriously unlink themselves, one apparently passing through the other.

① PREPARATION: Lay one silk out flat and tie two opposite corners
② together. Fold these opposite sides of the silk in toward each other, hiding the knot.

Put the handkerchief in your breast pocket, letting one end stick out.

PERFORMANCE: Show another silk of a different color, and tie two corners together, forming a circle.

Pull the prepared silk from your pocket. Thread it through the
③ first silk and tie its two ends together. This time you tie the false knot pictured.
④ Put right end A on end B.
⑤ Pull end B down with right thumb and forefinger.
⑥ Right thumb and forefinger grasp end A.
⑦ Left thumb and forefinger grasp end B.
⑧ Tie ends A and B in a single knot.
⑨ Pull knot tight.

You have, to all appearances, tied a square knot.
⑩ Lower the linked silks into a hat. Blow your magic whistle, or make a magic pass above the hat. Then reach in, pull the false knot apart, bring out the first silk, spread the circle, showing that it is still tied, then toss it to someone to examine.
⑪ Reach into the hat again, spread the center folds of the remaining silk, find the hidden knot, and lift this silk out and show it in the same way.

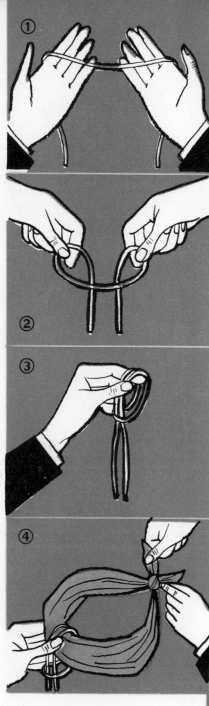

## THE HOUDINI HANDKERCHIEF

A handkerchief passes visibly through a rope.

Toss a silk handkerchief to a spectator. *"Please make sure that this contains no trap doors, mirrors, or concealed assistants."*

Hold a four-foot length of rope at the center so that it lies ① across the fingers of both hands, which are palm up.

Turn both hands over toward each other, forming a double loop. ②

*"Here is a pair of handcuffs."* Twist the loops again in the same ③ direction and place one loop on the other.

Ask the spectator to thread one end of the handkerchief through ④ both loops and then tie the ends of the handkerchief together. *"Make as many knots as you like—tight ones."*

Grasp the right end of the rope with the right hand about a ⑤ foot from the handkerchief, and take the other end of the rope in the same way with the left hand. *"Notice that the harder the rope is pulled the tighter the handcuffs grasp the handkerchief."* Jerk the hands apart forcefully so that the rope is pulled out into a straight line running through the handkerchief. Instead of the rope being looped about the handkerchief, the latter is now looped around the rope.

Have two spectators hold the ends of the rope and ask them to ⑥ wrap the rope once around their hands so they won't drop it. *"This handkerchief was once owned by Houdini, and it can escape as quickly as he did. Watch!"*

Take hold of the handkerchief at the center of the horizontal ⑦ fold and pull it, gently at first, until it loosens.

Then pull the silk quickly away from the rope. It appears to ⑧ pass right through the rope. Open the handkerchief out, showing that it is still tied in a circle.

Another very effective way to remove the silk is to thread a second shorter rope into the handkerchief knot. Hold an end of the rope in each hand and pull. The handkerchief leaves the spectator's rope and now encircles the rope you hold.

**MATERIALS**
Silk handkerchief
2 foot length of rope
4 foot length of rope

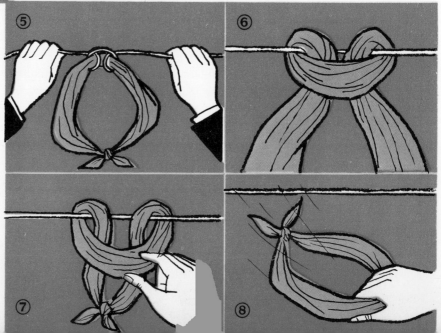

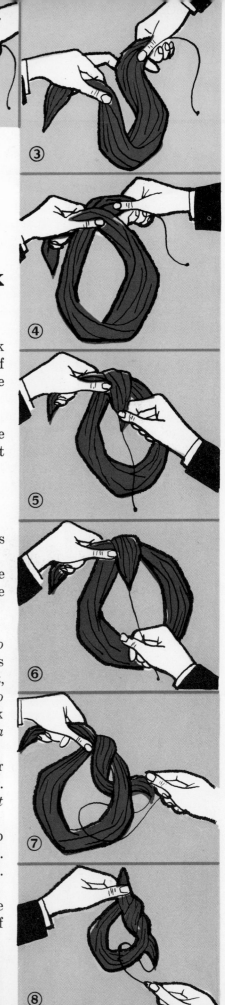

**MATERIALS**
Dark blue silk
handkerchief
18 inch length of
fine black silk thread

## THE SELF-UNTYING SILK

A knot tied in the center of a silk visibly unties itself.

① PREPARATION: Tie one end of an 18-inch length of very fine black silk thread to one corner of a silk. Tie a knot at the other end of the thread. Use a dark blue silk so that the thread will not be visible against it.

② PERFORMANCE: Hold the silk at diagonally opposite corners, the threaded end between the thumb and index finger of the right hand. The thread passes through the curled right fingers.

③ Move your right hand forward and toward the left.

④ Grasp the crossed corners of the silk with the left fingers.

⑤ Pull the threaded corner of the silk down.

⑥ Slide your right hand down along the thread until it reaches the knot.

⑦ Reach into the loop with this hand from the spectators' side and pull the corner through the loop, forming a loose knot in the center of the silk.

⑧ Let the silk hang from your left hand.

Look at the spectators and say, "*This is a very difficult knot to untie.*" As you say this, move your left hand upward. This causes the lower corner of the silk to curl up and pass through the knot, untying it. Pretend not to notice it, and continue, "*I am going to give a prize to anyone who can untie . . .*" Now look at the silk and appear to be surprised. "*That's odd. I could swear I tied a knot in that thing.*"

Tie the knot again. "*I am going to give a prize . . .*" Lift your hand again, quickly this time, and the knot unties itself rapidly.

Scowl at the silk. "*I'm sorry. I don't seem to be tying that knot right. I'll have to practice some more.*"

Put the silk aside, and then later in your program, pick it up again, scowl at it, and scratch your head as if you were puzzled. Tie the knot once more, and it unties itself again. Shake your head. "*I can't figure out what's wrong.*"

If you do this in artificial light and wear a dark jacket, the thread can't be seen. Don't try it if there is too much light or if you are wearing a white shirt and no jacket.

# THE MAGIC DYE TUBE

Silk handkerchiefs change color simply by being pushed through a paper tube. This is one of the prettiest and best of all silk tricks.

① PREPARATION: Cut a sheet of thin black cardboard or construction paper about 10″ by 12″ into the shape shown.

② Roll the projecting tab into a cylinder and cement it in position as shown. The cylinder should be slightly shorter than the width of your hand and about one inch in diameter, large enough so that two of your silks will fit into it. Cut two slits in the sides of

③ the tube, and put the ends of a length of cloth tape through the

④ slits. Secure the ends with black adhesive electrician's tape.

Roll the sheet around the tube and keep it in that condition with rubber bands so that whenever it is opened out it will curl back and re-form a cylinder around the inner tube. Load the inner tube with two colored silks.

⑤ PERFORMANCE: Pick up the tube with the left hand, concealed gimmick at the bottom. Open it out with the right hand and display it as shown here, the right hand covering the inner tube.

⑥ Let the sheet roll into a cylinder again, then push two white silks, one at a time, into the bottom of the cylinder. This pushes the concealed silks to the opposite end of the cylinder and when

⑦ you take them out they have been magically dyed in bright colors.

Unroll the cylinder once more and show it empty, your hand hiding the inner tube as before.

**MATERIALS**
Scissors
Sheet of thin black cardboard or construction paper
Rubber cement
Cloth tape
2 white silk handkerchiefs
2 silk handkerchiefs (different colors)
Black adhesive electrician's tape
Rubber bands

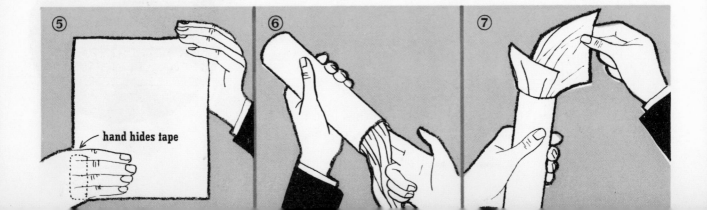

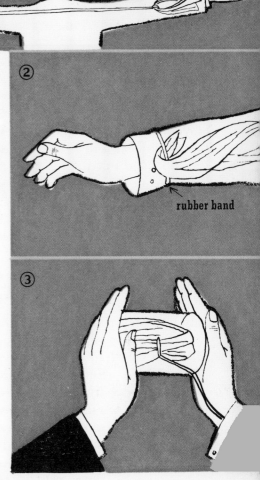

rubber band

## THE VISIBLE VANISH

The most magical of all tricks are those in which the magic happens in full view. Here, a silk handkerchief visibly and instantly vanishes from a glass tumbler.

① PREPARATION: The secret gimmick that accomplishes this is a stout piece of wrapping cord. Make a loop at one end with a slip knot and place this around the left wrist outside your shirtsleeve and just above the shirt cuff. When both arms are fully extended straight forward, the cord should go from your left wrist, up the coat sleeve, across your back, and down your right coat sleeve as far as your elbow. This end is tied around the center of a silk handkerchief.

Adjust the length of the cord so that you can hold the center of the silk in the right hand when the arms are bent at the elbows, and both hands are about six inches in front of your body. Let go of the silk and extend both arms straight forward. The center of the silk should be drawn up to the right elbow, and the ends of the silk should be out of sight about three inches up the right sleeve.

PERFORMANCE: This makes a fine opening trick because it is so quick and startling that it will make your audience sit up and take notice. With the pull in position, all you need to do is pull the silk down out of the sleeve, hold it at the center, your fingers covering the cord, put a glass tumbler in your left hand and make your entrance.

② The trick can also be done later during your performance this way. Put a rubber band around your right wrist just above the shirt cuff and tuck the ends of the silk in under it.

The tumbler is on your table and contains a duplicate silk. At the end of a previous trick, turn away from the audience, go to the tumbler and stand in front of it, hiding it. Put the duplicate silk out of sight in your shirt pocket, then pull the silk from your sleeve, and hold it in your right hand. Pick up the glass and face front again. Believing the handkerchief you hold to be the same one they saw earlier, the spectators will not suspect that it is attached to anything.

Look at the tumbler and say, *"Did you ever see a haunted drinking glass? Watch!"*

③ Push the silk into the glass, then place your right hand over the mouth of the glass, your left hand over the bottom, and hold the glass horizontally.

*"Keep your eyes on it. One! Two! Three! Go!"* As you say *"Go!"* lift the heel of your hand slightly, and jerk both arms forward and upward very quickly.

The silk, drawn up the sleeve in a flash, vanishes instantly. It's as close to looking like real magic as anything you can do.

**MATERIALS**
Stout wrapping cord
2 silk handkerchiefs
Glass tumbler
Rubber band

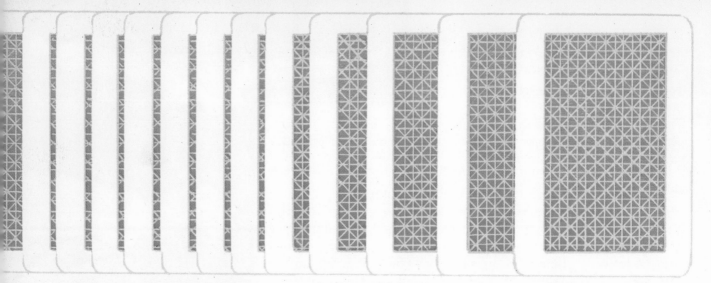

# Conjuring With Cards

### IMPROMPTU TRICKS

Some of the most mysterious and most entertaining of all magic tricks are those done with a deck of playing cards.

Except when you are challenged to use a borrowed deck, avoid cards which have been used for playing; they are often soiled, sticky, bent, and hard to handle. Get a deck of your own and save it for your magic. Better, get three decks all alike. You will sometimes want to exchange one deck secretly for another, and the third deck is useful for making special faked cards. The cards should be of the type which have white margins around the outside edges of the back design because this is important in some tricks.

IMPORTANT: *Have a deck of cards in your hands as you read the instructions that follow and do each action as it is described. This makes the explanations easier to understand and helps you learn the trick much faster.*

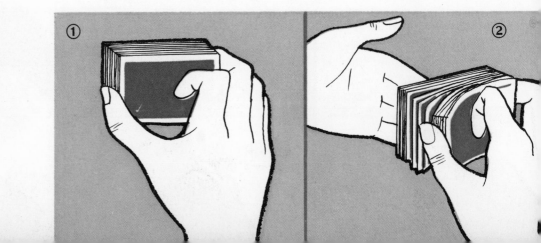

If you don't already know how, the very first thing you should learn is the proper way to shuffle. There are two methods and you should be able to do both.

## THE OVERHAND SHUFFLE

Place the deck on your left hand and tip the fingers up slightly so that the deck is at a forty-five degree angle. Grasp the ends of the deck with your right hand, between the thumb at the inner end and the middle fingers at the outer end.

①    Lift the deck upward but press against the top of the deck with your left thumb so that a few cards are drawn off and remain in your left hand.

②    Lower the cards in the right hand down onto those in the left hand and draw off several more cards with the left thumb. Continue this action, moving the right hand up and down and pulling off cards with the left thumb until they are all in the left hand. Practice this until you can do it smoothly and fairly fast.

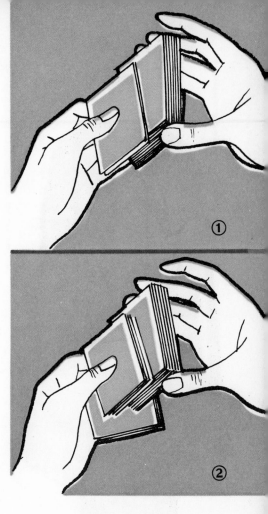

## THE RIFFLE SHUFFLE

This is the shuffle most card players use, but they usually do it with the deck resting on the table. Since you will often do your tricks while you are standing before your audience, you should learn to do it without using the table.

①    Place your right hand above the face-down deck. Put your thumb at the inner end, bend your index finger inward on top of the deck, and curl the ends of your other fingers around the deck's outer end.

②    Squeeze the deck and let about half the cards riffle off the end of your thumb onto the tips of your left fingers. Then put your
③ left forefinger between the two halves of the deck.

④    Lift the right hand, tilting the bottom half of the deck up and over to the left so that its right edge can be grasped by the left thumb.

    Each hand now holds half the deck in exactly the same way.
⑤ Place the ends held by the thumbs close together and let the cards riffle off the thumbs so that they interlace.

    Push both hands toward each other, shoving the two halves of the deck into each other. Then square up the cards.

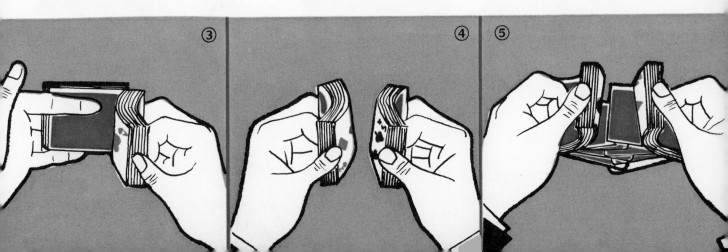

## THE KEY CARD

In a great many card tricks a spectator chooses a card, replaces it among the others, and the magician finds it, apparently by some magical means. He often does this in a very simple way. He gets a quick, secret look at some other card and then has the unknown chosen card replaced in the deck next to the card he knows. This known card is called a key, or locator, card. The important thing is to get a look at it secretly and without being suspected. Here are three good ways to do this.

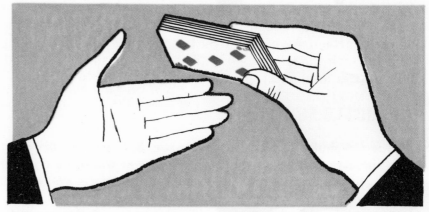

## THE GLIMPSE

Give the deck to a spectator to be shuffled. When you take it again, grasp it with your right hand, thumb underneath and fingers on top. As you bring the deck back to put it in your left hand, and *while your right hand is in motion*, tilt the deck just enough so that you get a quick glimpse of the face of the bottom card.

Another way is to wait until the deck is in the left hand, then turn it into a vertical position and tap the end of the deck on the table to square the cards. A quick downward glance as you do this enables you to glimpse the bottom card.

One of the very best ways to sight the card is to do it during the riffle shuffle. Note (page 53) that just after the deck is cut, the cards are held in such a way that the bottom card of the packet in the right hand can be seen. Simply let this card fall first as you begin to riffle so that it becomes the bottom card of the deck.

Next, to mislead anyone who may suspect that you have glimpsed a card, use one of the false shuffles described.

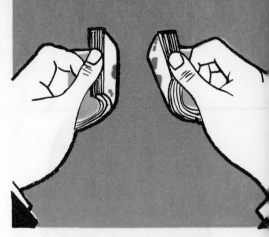

## FALSE RIFFLE SHUFFLE

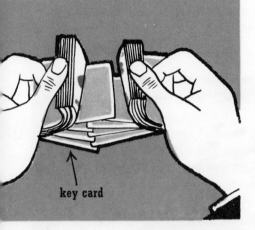

key card

When you cut the deck into two halves in order to riffle them together, your known key card is at the bottom of the packet of cards in your left hand. Simply begin the riffle by letting this card fall first, and shuffle all the other cards onto it.

## FALSE OVERHAND SHUFFLE

When your right thumb pulls some cards off the top of the deck as you begin the overhand shuffle, pull one or more cards off the bottom of the deck at the same time with your left fingers, thus keeping the key card on the bottom.

key card

## A FALSE CUT

If you also give the deck a false cut after the false shuffle, this makes it seem even more impossible that you could know the name or location of any card. Hold the deck on the palm of your left hand. Grasp the inner end of the deck at the sides between the right thumb and middle fingers. Pull the lower half of the deck out and drop it on top of the cards in the left hand. This is a fair cut which buries the bottom card in the middle of the deck. The false cut is done the same way except for one thing. Squeeze the deck gently with the left hand as you pull out the lower half. This holds the bottom card in place and keeps it in the left hand on the bottom of the deck.

Now let's do a trick.

# THE POINTING FINGER

A spectator chooses a card and returns it to the deck during a shuffle. The performer spreads the cards face up, runs his forefinger back and forth over them, and stops mysteriously on the chosen card.

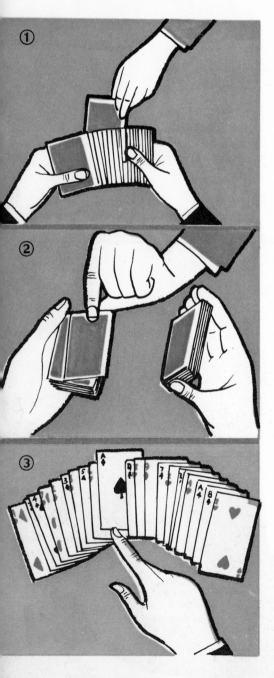

Secretly get a glimpse of the card on the bottom of the deck by one of the methods explained. Shuffle and cut the deck, keeping this key card on the bottom.

① Start pushing the cards from the left hand into the right hand and ask a spectator to take one out. Tell him to look at it, remember it, and also show it to anyone else who is watching. This last instruction is always good because sometimes the spectator who chooses a card forgets what it was.

Then begin to shuffle the deck overhand and say, "*Tell me when to stop.*" When the spectator tells you to stop, hold out the cards in your left hand, ask him to put his card on top of them, and ② then drop the remaining cards in your right hand on top. This has put the bottom key card, whose name you know, directly on top of his card.

Square the cards. Lift about half the cards off the deck and place them under the lower half. This is called a single cut. Do it twice.

Turn the deck face up and spread the cards out in a row. As you do this, look for your key card. The spectator's chosen card will be the card just above it. You could point out his card at once, but don't. A magic trick should never look easy; do a little acting and pretend that it is very difficult. Like this.

Tell the spectator, "*I will try to read your mind. I'll run my finger across the cards and when it points at your card, think the word 'Stop!' Don't say anything. Just think.*"

Run your finger slowly across the cards without stopping. Look at the spectator. "*No, you're not thinking hard enough. All I get is static. Try again.*"

This time stop shortly after you have gone past his card. "*That's better. You just thought 'Stop!', but you are a slow thinker. I went past it.*"

Move your finger back toward his card, go past it again, then go back and forth slowly, and finally say, "*There! You just thought 'Stop!' It came in very clearly.*" And bring your finger ③ down directly on the chosen card.

As soon as you have learned this trick you will be able to do the next three. They are all done the same way, but they all end differently, and from the spectator's point of view, they all seem to be different tricks.

# THE LUCKY HUNCH

The performer deals the cards one at a time and stops just *before* he turns up the chosen card without ever having seen it.

**MATERIALS**
**Deck of playing cards**

You begin, as in "The Pointing Finger" trick, by secretly glimpsing the bottom card and then retaining it on the bottom during a shuffle and cut. You could also have the card selected and returned to the deck in the same way, but it is more deceptive if you vary the procedure.

This time put the deck in front of the spectator and give him these instructions. *"Cut the deck into three piles. Then look at and remember the top card of any pile, and replace it on any pile."*

You know that your key card is the bottom card of the pile that was on the bottom of the deck, and you now see to it that the key card goes on top of the spectator's card. If he puts his chosen card back on the pile that contains the key card, tell him to cut the pile (this puts your key card on his card). Then have him put this pile on either of the other piles, and put the third pile on top of both.

If he puts his card on one of the other piles, point to the pile containing the key card and say, *"Put this pile on your card, and the last pile on both."* Again, your key card is on the chosen card.

Tell him to cut the deck. He may do this two or three times, provided they are all single cuts.

This all seems very fair because the spectator cut the deck into piles himself, chose any one of the top cards, put it back on any pile, and reassembled the deck himself. You haven't touched the cards at all and the chosen card seems to have been lost among the others, leaving no clue as to its whereabouts. Actually you have your secret clue—the key card.

Now take the deck, and begin dealing off cards one at a time, face up. *"I feel lucky today, and if you will concentrate on your card, I think I can stop dealing as soon as it appears."* This sounds difficult, but you do even better.

Stop dealing as soon as you turn up the key card. *"I've got a hunch that this next card which I haven't even looked at yet is your card."* Take it off the deck but keep it face down. *"Name your card, please."* The spectator does so, and you turn up the card you hold, showing that it is his. *"Only a magician could be that lucky!"*

## THE MAGICIAN'S MISTAKE

The performer makes a mistake, but just as the spectators are about to enjoy a laugh at his expense, the tables are turned and they find that the laugh is on them.

**MATERIALS**
**Deck of playing cards**

Do "The Lucky Hunch" trick first, and then offer to repeat it. This sets things up so that the spectators will fall into the trap you are about to set. Repeat everything just as before until you start to deal the cards.

Then say, *"I'm not always that lucky, but don't say anything if I miss. I always know when I'm wrong."* Deal the cards in an overlapping row so that none of them are completely covered. When your key card shows up, deal off the next card—the chosen one—and keep going. Deal four or five more cards.

Push the next card over with your thumb as though you were about to deal it off—and stop suddenly. Look at the spectators. *"This is really my lucky day. I am so sure that the very next card I turn over will be the one you chose that I'll buy everybody here an ice cream soda if I'm wrong. Anybody want to bet?"*

Since they all see that you have gone past the card and they think that you are going to turn up the next card on the deck, they will probably all accept the bet gleefully.

Then you reach down, pick up the chosen card, and turn it face down. *"I'll turn this one over. Now everybody owes me an ice cream soda!"*

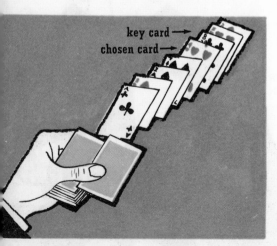

key card →
chosen card →

The performer lets a spectator do this trick himself, and, although he has never done any magic before, he succeeds! He deals one card for each letter of his name and the card he chose turns up on the last letter.

Once again you secretly glimpse the bottom card and see that it goes onto the spectator's chosen card when he replaces it in the deck. Give the deck several single cuts.

"*If you think of your card real hard and broadcast nice, clear thought waves, I can sometimes run through the deck and find it at once.*"

Turn the deck so that you can see the faces, run through the cards and look for your key card. When you find it, begin spelling your own first name mentally, and push one card over to the right for each letter. Start the spell with the key card.

When you finish spelling, separate the cards at that point, look up and make a gesture toward the spectator with your right hand and the cards it holds. Say, "*You're not concentrating well at all.*" Then replace the cards in your right hand *under* those in the left hand. Square the deck and turn it face down.

"*We'll have to try something else. When I have trouble reading someone's mind I usually do this. Suppose I'm looking for the _____ of _____.*" (Here you name your key card.) "*I wave my hand three times around the deck like this, then spell my name, dealing one card for each letter.*" Do this, then say, "*This always works.*" Turn the last card dealt face up, showing that it is the one you named.

Put all the dealt-off cards back on the *bottom* of the deck (the chosen card is now on top of the deck). Tell the spectator, "*It's not hard. You try it.*" Give him the deck, and have him deal one card face down for each letter as he spells his own name.

When he finishes spelling his first name, tell him that he can also spell his last name if he likes, and even his middle name. Since you may not know his middle name, the final climax becomes even more surprising if he does spell it.

When he finishes spelling and turns up the last card, look surprised and say, "*That's not your card.*" Then add, "*Oh, I know what happened. You didn't make the magic pass.*" He usually has forgotten this because you didn't remind him to do it. If he did remember to do it, you merely tell him that he did it too slow or too fast.

His chosen card is now on the bottom of the pile he dealt off. Pick these up all together, put them back on the deck, and ask him to try again. Take his hand in yours and wave it three times around the deck to make sure he does it correctly. Then tell him to spell his name again.

When he reaches the last card, stop him, have him name his chosen card, then let him turn it up himself. He has succeeded. Congratulate him. "*I never saw anyone learn magic so quickly.*"

Then ask him, "*Will you promise not to tell anyone else how you did that?*" The look on his face, since he doesn't know how he did it, always gets a laugh.

**YOUR MAGIC NAME**

## THE CARD FROM THE HAT

A card is chosen and shuffled back into the deck which is placed in a man's hat. On command the selected card jumps from the hat.

Hold the deck in your left hand and riffle the outer ends of the cards with your right fingers. Tell a spectator to stick his finger ① into the deck at any time. When he does so, lift off all the cards above his finger and lower them to your side. Then, as the spectator takes the card on which his finger rests, squeeze the ② packet in your right hand at the ends, bending the cards upward at the middle.

The spectator looks at his card, remembers it, and replaces it where it was. Slap the right-hand packet carelessly down on top of his card and square the deck. The bend in the top cards leaves an ③ opening in the side of the deck.

Cut the deck at this break and put the lower group of cards on top, thus bringing the chosen card to the top. Riffle shuffle once or twice keeping the top card on top. Give the deck a false cut.

Take a man's hat, the crown of which is creased. Hold it brim up and put the deck in it. The crease in the hat divides it into two sections. Put the deck in the section nearest the audience, lift off the top card and place it by itself in the rear section.

Hold up the hat, ask the spectator to name his card, then snap your forefinger off your thumb so that it hits the outside of the ④ hat just below the chosen card. One card jumps high out of the hat, and proves to be the card that was named.

## THE LIE DETECTOR I

A spectator selects a card at random behind the performer's back and the latter finds it while his back is still turned.

Once again secretly glimpse the bottom card of the deck (preferably after a spectator has shuffled the deck). Then give the deck an overhand shuffle, and as you reach the last few cards pull them down into the left hand one at a time so that the last card (your key card) is left on top.

Practice this until you can do it without having to watch the deck. In fact, don't ever look at the deck when you are shuffling unless you are sighting the bottom card during the riffle shuffle, and then look down only briefly at just the right moment. If you pay no attention to the shuffle yourself, the audience won't watch it carefully either.

After the key card has been shuffled to the top, cut off about half the deck and hand it to a spectator. "*After I turn my back, I want you to deal off some cards one at a time, face down, into a pile. Like this.*" Deal off a few cards from those you hold so that he sees exactly what he is to do.

**MATERIALS**
Deck of playing cards
Man's hat

Turn your back, and add, *"Deal them silently so I can't hear how many you deal. Whenever you get tired, stop, and let me know that you have finished."*

When he has done this tell him, *"Look at the top card on the packet you still hold, then put all the dealt-off cards back on it."* (This puts the key card on his card.)

*"Magicians,"* you continue, *"are very difficult people to fool. I want you to try to fool me. Deal the cards face up, one at a time, and call out the name of each card aloud. But when your card turns up, lie about it. Call it something else. And keep going. Even though I can't see your face I think I can tell when you are fibbing."*

He does this and you listen for the name of your key card. Then, when he names the next card, turn suddenly, point at him dramatically and say, *"You're lying!"*

MATERIALS
Deck of playing cards

## THE CARD THROUGH THE TABLE

A spectator chooses a card and it is returned to the deck. The performer places the deck on the table and bangs his fist down on it. The chosen card leaves the deck and passes down through the table.

MATERIALS
Deck of playing cards
Plate or napkin

① Hold the deck in your left hand and grasp it from above with the right hand, thumb at the inner end, fingers at the outer end. Riffle the outer ends of the deck. Ask a spectator to tell you when to stop. Stop at his command, lift off all the cards held by the right hand, and tilt them up so the spectators can see the card on the bottom of the packet. Tell them to remember the card and concentrate on it.

As they do this, tip your left hand up and back slightly to hide the top of the packet it holds. Squeeze the inner end of the packet so that the cards receive a concave bend.

② After the selected card has been noted, lower the right hand and quickly slap the packet it holds down on the one in the left hand. Square the cards neatly. The bending of the cards has left a break in the deck at the inner end only.

Cut the deck, lifting off all the cards above the break. Don't look at the end of the deck to find the break. Cut to it by feel. If you lift all the deck a half inch or so with your right hand, thumb at the inner end, then release the pressure of your thumb slightly, all the cards below the break will drop off automatically. Place the top portion of the deck under the other cards, completing the cut.

This brings the chosen card to the bottom. Quickly give the deck an overhand shuffle, retaining the bottom card on the bottom as explained on page 55.

①

②

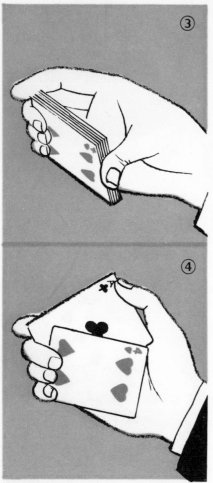

Now put a plate (or a folded napkin) in the center of the table and put the deck face down on it.

"*I am,*" you announce, "*going to make the chosen card penetrate all the cards under it and keep going down through the plate. And just to make sure that I didn't sneak the card under the plate already, will someone please look.*"

As you say this, pick up the deck again. Hold it in your right hand from above, with the thumb at the inner end. The outer end of the deck rests against the first joint of your index finger and against the second joints of the other fingers. The first joints of the other fingers are curled in under the deck.

Bring this hand and the deck back and down to the edge of the table. At the same time, twist the fingers to the right under the deck so that the bottom card swivels out to the right on an angle. As your right hand reaches the table's edge and goes very slightly below it, straighten these fingers, letting the bottom card drop into your lap.

This can all be done while the others are looking under the plate. Bring your right hand back to the table edge slowly, drop the card at once, and then replace the deck on the plate.

Square the deck neatly, using both hands and making it obvious, without saying so, that both hands are empty. Close your right hand into a fist, count, "*One! Two! Three! Go!*" and bring it down hard on the deck. "*I think that did it.*"

Ask someone to remove the deck, and look under the plate. He finds nothing. "*That's funny,*" you say. "*It has always worked before. Perhaps I hit the deck too hard.*"

Reach down with your left hand, take the card from your lap, and reach out under the table. "*That's just what happened! It went right through the plate and almost all the way through the table.*" Jerk downward as though you were pulling it loose, then bring it up and toss it on the table face up.

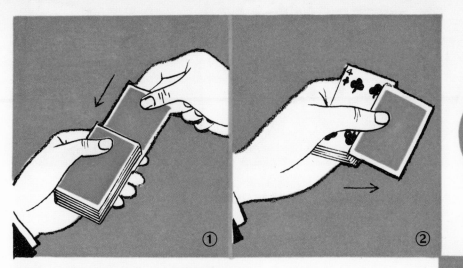

## THE ONE-ARMED MAGICIAN

A spectator chooses a card, replaces it in the deck, and the performer finds it almost instantly while the deck is behind his back and he is using only one hand.

After a spectator has shuffled the deck, spread the cards before him and ask him to remove one. *"But don't look at it until I turn my back. I want you to be sure that I can't see it."*

Turn your back. While he notes the card and shows it to the other spectators, turn the deck face up, and then turn the top card face down on the others. Don't look down at the cards while you do this, and keep your arms pressed against your sides so that there is no telltale movement of your elbows.

Face your audience again and ask the person holding the card to push its corner into the end of the deck anywhere he likes. Then you push the card in flush with the others.

Now square the deck carefully and place it on your left hand, which you hold perfectly flat with the fingers outstretched. You do this to convince everyone that the chosen card is flush with the others and that you can't possibly be keeping one finger under it.

*"I couldn't have seen your card, but I am going to try to find it —with one hand only."* Put your right hand in your pocket. *"While the deck is behind my back."* Put the deck behind your back. *"And in the world record time of less than three seconds! This is one of the most difficult feats in all magic!"*

As soon as the deck is out of sight behind your back, move the top card to the right with your thumb, push up against it with your left fingertips and turn it over. Then turn the whole deck over, and bring it into view again.

Ask the spectator to name his card, and after he does, say, *"Yes, that's what I thought."* Begin pushing the face-down cards off the top of the deck onto the table or floor. *"That's the card I found with one hand, and turned face up!"*

The chosen card is found to be face up. Since he himself replaced it upside down, although he didn't know it, it can't be anything else.

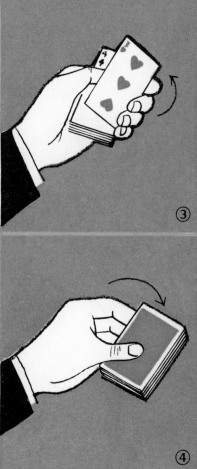

## THE SPECTATOR MAGICIAN

A spectator finds his own chosen card in a surprising and impossible manner without knowing how he did it.

Point to a spectator. *"I'll show you how to become a magician in one easy lesson, no charge. Take the deck and give it a good shuffle."* Then tell him, *"Give me about half the deck—either half."* Now turn your back. *"I won't look. Cut your cards once, then look at the top card, let the others see it, and put it back on top."*

While he is doing that, secretly turn the *bottom* card of the packet you hold face up, and then turn the card that is *second* from the top face up. Square the packet neatly.

Face your audience again, and put your cards on his cards. *"Now since you are going to do this trick, come up here on the stage."* Have him face the audience, and see that he is holding the deck face down in his hand in the usual position for dealing.

*"Since this is the first magic you have ever done we'll make it very difficult. Put both hands behind your back. Now slide off the top card and push it into the middle of the deck. You've done that? Good. Now turn the top card of the deck. You've done that? Good. Now . . ."* Stop as though you just remembered something. *"I'm very sorry. I almost ruined everything. I forgot the most important part. I didn't tell you that you must think of the card you chose just as hard as you can. It'll never work if you don't. Do that please."*

Put your ear near his head and listen. *"That's fine. I can hear the wheels going around. Now, turn the top card of the deck over so that it is face up, and then push it, face up, into the middle of the deck."* (What he doesn't know, since he is doing this behind his back, is that this second card is already face up. He is really putting it into the deck face down.)

Now ask him to hold the deck so that everyone can see it, and run through the cards until he comes to a face-up card. *"If you pushed that face-up card into the deck behind your back right next to the card you were thinking of—that would be a miracle. What was your card?"*

As he names it, reach over and slowly pull out the card lying directly under the face-up card. Peek at the card as though you don't believe this could happen, then look surprised. *"By golly, he did it!"* Turn the card so everyone can see it, then ask the spectator to take a bow and you lead the applause.

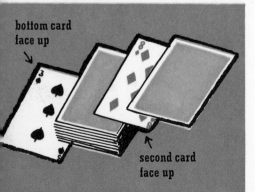

bottom card face up

second card face up

④      ⑤

**two cards held as one**

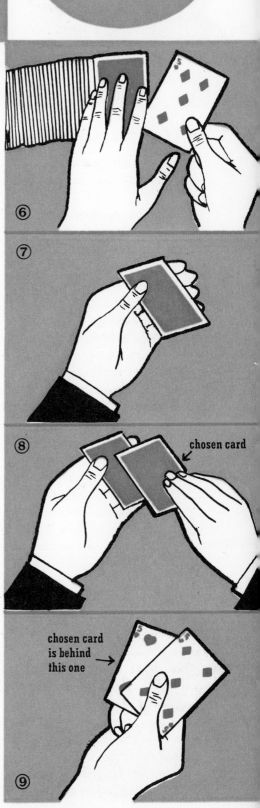

**MATERIALS**
**Deck of playing cards**

⑥

⑦

⑧    **chosen card**

⑨    **chosen card is behind this one**

## COINCIDENCE

The performer removes a card from the deck, then a spectator takes one. The denomination and color of both cards prove to be the same.

(1)   Shuffle and cut the deck, then hold it so that it faces you. Note the card in front and, as you begin to push the cards from your left to right hand, slide the front card down about a half inch.

Continue pushing cards over to the right until you find the card that matches the front card in both denomination and color. For example, if the front card is a red five, find the other red five.

(2)   Separate the deck at this point and slide the matching card in front of the front card.

Then push the cards together, squaring them at the sides.

(3)   Hold the deck in the left hand, thumb along the left side, all four fingers along the side.

(4)   Push upward against the bottom edge of the projecting cards with the right thumb until both are squarely lined up one on the other. Then grasp both cards between the thumb and forefinger

(5)   of the right hand and lift them off the deck, holding them as though they were one card.

(6)   Turn the rest of the deck face down with your left hand and spread the cards out in a line on the table or floor.

Put both cards, as one, into your left hand, holding them at the

(7)   side edges. Ask a spectator to push any one of the face-down cards forward away from the others. Make sure he realizes that this is an absolutely free choice.

While everyone is watching him do this, bring your right hand up to your mouth for a second and moisten the ball of your thumb by touching it to the tip of your tongue.

(8)   Then pick up the selected card, placing your thumb beneath it, and transfer some of the moisture to its face. Without looking at it, put it on the cards in your left hand, and align them together. Say, "*I knew you would take that one.*"

Take the three cards with your right hand, your thumb underneath, fingers on top. Turn them to face yourself and at the same time slide your thumb to the right, spreading the cards. The

(9)   chosen card will stick to the back of one of the others and you appear to hold only two cards.

"*This proves it. I took one that matches.*" Turn your hand and show that both cards are alike.

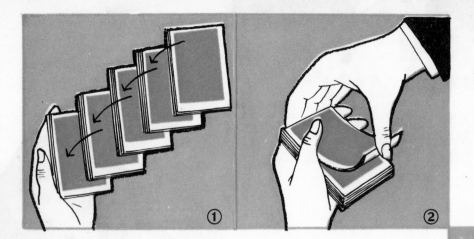

## MENTAL SELECTION

Several spectators merely think of cards and yet the performer finds them all without ever seeing the faces of any of the cards.

Have someone shuffle the deck. Then give five spectators five cards each and put the rest of the deck aside. "*Look at your cards,*" you tell them. "*Select one mentally and remember it. Then turn them face down.*"

① When this has been done, go to the first spectator on your left and take his cards face down in your left hand. Move across to the right, having each packet replaced on the preceding one. Number each spectator in your mind as being No. 1, 2, 3, 4, and 5.

When you have collected all the cards, put your right hand over them, fingers at the outer end, thumb at the inner end, and square them up. Then draw everyone's attention to your face by saying, "*Five people have selected cards mentally. I will now try to find the cards you are thinking of.*" As you say this, your right thumb

② pulls a few of the top cards upward at the inner end, bending them.

Hold the cards as though you are about to begin an overhand shuffle. Lift about half the cards off the bottom with your right hand and throw them on top. Do this three or four times. This actually gives the deck a series of single cuts, but if you do it casually and rather fast it will look like a shuffle.

③ Now glance down at the cards and notice the opening in the side edge of the deck made by the bent cards. Separate the packet at this opening and throw the bottom cards on top.

This brings the bent cards to the top and all the cards are now back in their original position. Square the cards again and give them all a quick downward bend which straightens out the bent cards.

④ Deal five cards in a row from left to right, then five more cards on these in the same manner, and continue dealing until you have five piles of five cards each.

Pick up any one of the piles, spread the cards so the spectators can see their faces. "*Does anyone see the card he is thinking of?*"

If the first spectator on your left, whom you have remembered as being No. 1, says he sees his card, this tells you that the top card in the group you hold, the first card on the right, is his. If spectator No. 2 sees his card, it is the second from the right. The ⑤ third spectator's card would be third from the right, and so on.

Suppose spectator No. 3 sees his card in this group. Pretend to concentrate, ask him to do the same, then have him hold his hand out palm up. You don't want him to know yet whether or not you have found the right card because you are saving this for the grand climax. Square the cards; cover them with your right hand so that he can't see which one you remove. Take out the third card from the top and put it face down on his hand. "*Don't look at it yet.*"

Pick up another pile; ask if anyone sees his card. As soon as someone replies, you know which one it is. Remove it and have him hold it.

If no one sees his card among the five shown, as sometimes happens, simply throw this group aside and continue. This merely means that one of the remaining piles will contain two of the chosen cards.

When all five cards have been found, ask each person in turn to name his card aloud, then turn up the card he holds. Each person has the card he chose mentally.

You can also do this with four persons provided you give each one four cards, and then deal four piles. Or with six persons, if you give each six cards, and deal six piles.

# Prearranged Cards

## FOUR OF A KIND

A spectator chooses a card which is put aside without being looked at. The performer deals out three more cards, stopping at numbers called by the spectators. These three cards not only prove to be all of the same denomination, but they also match the first chosen card!

PREPARATION: Place four like cards (such as four jacks) on top of the deck. Then four more like cards (such as four sixes) on these. And, finally, any four assorted cards on top of these.

PERFORMANCE: Begin by giving the deck a false shuffle (page 55), and a false cut (page 55), which will not disturb these top twelve cards.

Deal out the four assorted cards in a row face up. Then change your mind. *"It would be better if we dealt the cards face down."* Gather the cards and put them aside face down.

① Deal four more cards in a row face down. Deal a second row of four cards face down.

Ask a spectator to choose either row. Gather up the other row and put these four cards aside on the four cards previously discarded.

Ask the spectator to touch one of the four cards. Put this card aside without showing its face.

Pick up the three cards that remain, put them back on the deck, and then pick up the eight discards and put these on top.

Point to the card the spectator chose. *"I'm going to show you how to find out the name of a card without looking at it. I'll deal some more cards and I want you to decide how many I should deal. Will someone please call out a number—not too big because that will take too long—any number between ten and twenty."*

② When a number is called (let's say 16), deal off that many cards one at a time. Then put the deck down and pick up the cards that were dealt.

*"Now we add the digits in the number you chose and deal that many cards back onto the deck."* (If the number was 16, add 1 and
③ 6 and deal 7 cards back onto the deck. If the number was 12, then 3 cards would be dealt back onto the deck. Always deal the cards one at a time.)

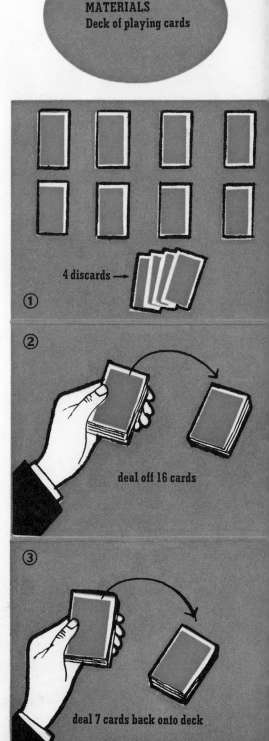

MATERIALS
Deck of playing cards

① 4 discards →

② deal off 16 cards

③ deal 7 cards back onto deck

put next card aside ④

put remaining cards
back on deck ⑤

⑥

"*Then we put the next card to one side.*" Put the top card of the ④
packet you hold to one side, and replace the remaining cards as a ⑤
group on the deck.

"*Now, we'll do that again as a double check. Will someone please
call another number between ten and twenty?*" Deal again in exactly the same way and put the card you arrive at to one side.
"*Just to make absolutely sure we get the right answer, let's have
a third number.*" Deal again as before and put a card aside.

"*Remember that you chose three different numbers at random.*"
You accent this fact because it makes what is to come seem to be
quite impossible. Actually, no matter what numbers are called,
dealing in this fashion always ends on the card that was ninth
from the top when the deal started, but no one ever stops to
figure this out; too much is happening.

You now have three cards laid out face down in addition to the
one originally chosen by the spectator. Turn the first of these three
cards face up. Suppose it is a jack. "*This tells us that the card you
chose is a jack.*" Turn up the second card, showing another jack.
"*This double-checks our answer.*" Turn up the third card, another ⑥
jack. "*And this proves it!*"

Ask the spectator who chose the first card to turn it up. He
finds that it is the fourth jack!

The fact that the spectators have such great freedom of choice,
both as to the first card chosen and the numbers called, makes
this surprising climax a real mystery.

## DECK SWITCH

In the two tricks that follow you must secretly exchange a deck
that has been shuffled for one that has been prearranged in a certain order. The easiest way to do this is to put a rubber band
around the prearranged deck at one end and carry it in your
jacket pocket.

Using another deck, do a trick or two during which the cards are
fairly shuffled, preferably by a spectator. Then put the deck in
your pocket (next to the prearranged deck), pretending that you
have finished with it and are about to do something else. Grasp
the second deck, push the rubber band off with your thumb, and
suddenly remember that you want to do another card trick. Bring
out the prearranged deck. If you do this casually, the spectators
will never suspect that the shuffled deck has been switched for
another one.

**MATERIALS**
2 Decks of playing cards
Rubber band

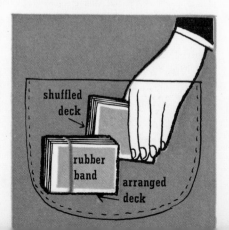

shuffled
deck

rubber
band

arranged
deck

## DOUBLE DISCOVERY

Two spectators each choose a card, then shuffle their cards back into the deck themselves. The performer finds both cards at the same time.

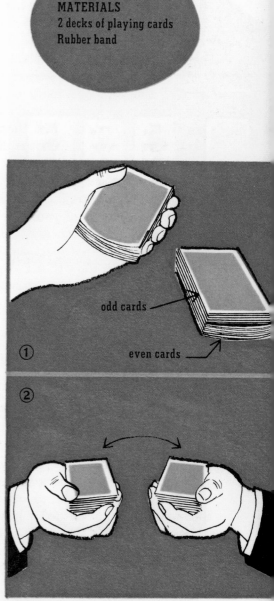

MATERIALS
2 decks of playing cards
Rubber band

PREPARATION: Deal the deck into two piles, putting all the even-numbered cards in one pile, the odd cards in another. The jacks and kings count as odd cards; the queen is even. Hold the even packet in your left hand and squeeze the sides slightly at the inner end only so that the cards bend upward at the corners. Do the same with the odd packet but bend the corners downward.
① Put this packet on the first one. This leaves an opening in the inner edge of the deck that separates the two halves.

Carry this deck in your pocket and then secretly exchange it for the deck you have been using, as explained previously under "Deck Switch" (page 70).

PERFORMANCE: Begin by announcing, "*I will now do two tricks at once.*" Cut the deck at the break and hold half in each hand. Ask two spectators to choose cards at the same time. One takes a card from the left-hand group, one from the right-hand group.

② "*I'll turn my back while you look at them.*" While your back is turned secretly transfer the left-hand group of cards to the right hand and vice versa.

Face the spectators again; give the cards in your left hand to the spectator on your left, the others to the spectator on your right. "*Replace your chosen cards and then shuffle.*" (Because you switched packets from hand to hand, the spectator who took an odd card is now shuffling it into the group of even-numbered cards, and the one who chose an even-numbered card has replaced his among the odd cards.)

When the shuffling is finished, ask each spectator to make sure his card is not on either the top or bottom. "*If it is, cut the cards so that yours is lost in the middle.*"

Take the cards, put one half on the other, and give the deck two or three single cuts. Turn the deck to face yourself, tell the first spectator to think of his card, and then look for the even-numbered card among the odd ones.

③ When you find it, take it and all the cards above it off with your right hand and point at the spectator. "*Are you sure you're thinking? I'm not getting a thing.*" Then replace the cards in your right hand *under* those in the left. (This puts one of the chosen cards at the bottom of the face-up deck.)

Turn to the second spectator. "*I hope you can do better.*" Now look for the odd card among the even ones. Take it out when you find it, but don't show it. Scowl at it, shake your head, and say, "*No, I don't think that's it.*" Put it back on the face of the deck.

Run through the cards again, remove one whose color matches the card on the face of the deck, and show it. "*I think this is the right color, but it's the wrong card.*" Put it back in the center of the deck.

"*People who haven't learned how to concentrate very well make things tough.*" Although you are pretending to have trouble, you have actually found both cards and have one on the face of the deck, one on the back. Turn the deck face down, cut it into two halves and riffle shuffle them together, letting the bottom card fall first, the top one last, so that the chosen cards remain in position. (This shuffle destroys the arrangement of the deck and leaves no clues for anyone who might want to take a look at it later.)

"*Well, I guess there's only one thing to do: I'll have to use real magic!*" Put your right hand to your mouth for a second and touch the tips of your forefinger and thumb with your tongue. Take the deck with your right hand, thumb on the face, forefinger on the back. Press firmly against the deck, hold the cards up high, and say, "*I'll try to find both cards at the same time—with one hand—in less than one second. Watch!*"

④ Bring the deck down above the left hand, turn it sideways, and release the pressure of your fingers slightly, letting all the cards, except the two on top and bottom, drop into your left hand. Spread the two cards apart, ask the spectators to name the cards they chose, then show that these are the ones you have.

If you have convinced everyone that things have gone wrong and that the trick is about to fail, this is a startling climax.

③                    ④

**MATERIALS**
2 decks of playing cards
Rubber band

## A NEW WORLD'S RECORD

When you do several tricks, the last one should always be a miracle that tops everything that has gone before. Here is a card trick that fills the bill. Several persons simultaneously choose cards and replace them in the deck anywhere they like. The performer promptly finds them all.

The deck you use is stacked in advance, the cards being separated into suits and each suit arranged in numerical order: 1, 2, 3, 4, 5, 6, 7, 8, 9, 10, jack, queen, king. Carry this prearranged deck in your pocket as explained under "Deck Switch," and, after you have done some other card trick during which the deck has been legitimately shuffled, switch decks.

Begin by announcing, "*Ladies and gentlemen, I will now attempt to break a world's record.*" Go to several people in turn and ask each to take a card from the deck.

Then spread the remaining cards in a line on the table face down, and step back away from the cards. Ask each person to come forward, one at a time, and push his card back in among the others wherever he likes.

When all the cards have been returned, close the spread and hold the deck as though about to begin an overhand shuffle. Pull up about half the cards from the bottom of the deck and throw them on top. Do this three or four times. If you do it carelessly and quickly it will pass for a shuffle. Then ask someone to cut the cards.

Turn the deck to face yourself, ask everyone to concentrate, and then run through and look for the cards that are out of sequence. As you come to each one, throw it out face down. When you find the last card, remember its name, but don't remove it. Instead, give the deck two or three good riffle shuffles, destroying your prearrangement. While you do this tell the spectators, "*You are all concentrating very well—all except you.*" Point to a boy. "*You've got just one thing on your mind—girls! Especially one girl! If you don't stop that and help me by thinking of your card I'll tell everyone who she is!*"

Run through the cards once more, find the card you remembered, and put it with the others. Put the deck aside, pick up the cards you removed, mix them a bit with an overhand shuffle, and then ask each person to name his card aloud. As each card is named, toss it out face up.

When only one card remains, say, "*I have just equaled the world's record for finding chosen cards simultaneously! If this last card is correct, I am the new world's champion!*" When it is named, show it dramatically, and take your bow.

# Prepared Cards

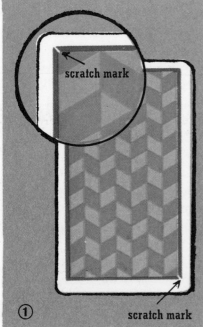

① scratch mark

scratch mark

**MATERIALS**
Deck of playing cards
Single edge razor blade
(Handle carefully!)

## THE ELECTRIC CARD

A chosen card is found by the performer although he never sees the faces of any of the cards.

PREPARATION: One card in your deck is marked on the back. Use the corner of a razor blade and scratch a small white mark in the ① ink of the back design in the upper left and lower right corners.

PERFORMANCE: Just before you begin this trick, turn the deck face up and say, *"I want to make sure the joker is not in the deck; this next trick won't work if it is."* When you come to the key card whose back is marked, lift it and all the cards above it off and put them under the remaining cards. Continue running through the cards. If there is a joker in the deck remove it; if not just say, *"Good. No joker."*

The marked card, when you hold the deck face down, is now on top of the deck, and you are ready to continue. Give the deck a riffle shuffle, letting the top card fall last so that it remains on top.

Spread the deck and ask someone to touch one. Take this card and all those above it off with the right hand. Put the lower half of the deck aside, square the right-hand half and show the touched card on its bottom to the spectators. Keep your head turned away so that it is obvious you can't see it.

Ask each person to take a good look at the card, and touch it for a second with his forefinger. *"This,"* you explain, *"charges the chosen card with electricity."*

Give these cards a cut (which puts the chosen card on your key card), then drop the packet on the deck, and cut the deck or allow a spectator to do so.

② Push six or seven cards off the top of the deck and hold them fanned in your right hand. Close your eyes; ask a spectator to concentrate on the chosen card and run his forefinger across the faces of the cards. *"If your card is in this group I'll know it because I'll get an electric shock."*

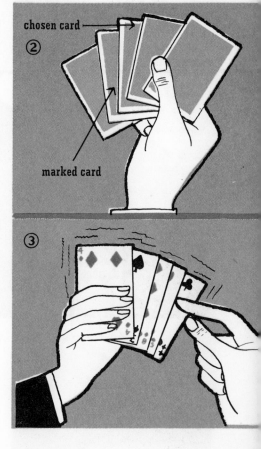

chosen card

②

marked card

Nothing happens the first time. Toss the cards aside and take off several more. Each time as you spread the cards off the top of the deck, watch for the marked card. You know, when you see it, that the card chosen is the one just *above* it. Mentally count from the chosen card over to the right so you know how many cards down it is from the top card.

③ Now, as soon as the spectator touches the cards, make them vibrate rapidly back and forth against the end of his finger, just as though an electric current had suddenly started flowing into your hand. The spectator sometimes jumps as though he had also received a shock.

③

Put the remainder of the deck down, take the fanned cards into the left hand, and square them up. Shake your right hand once or twice as though it still hurt. *"Gee! That must have been at least 120 volts!"*

Keep your eyes tightly closed during all this, then deal off cards one at a time and have a spectator touch each one. Since you know how far down the chosen card lies, you know when to receive another shock. As soon as this happens, drop the chosen card face up. *"I don't do this trick often,"* you say. *"It's too dangerous."*

If you have acted this out well, some spectators will even be afraid to pick up the chosen card when you ask them to hand it to you. And it is one of the most baffling tricks you can do because you never see the faces of any of the cards at any time.

## DIVINING KNIFE

The marked card used in the foregoing trick enables you to do "The Pointing Finger" trick (page 56) in an even more mysterious fashion, because you never see the faces of the cards.

At the beginning, your marked card is on the bottom of the face-down deck. A spectator removes a card from the deck. Begin an overhand shuffle and ask him to replace it. When he does so, drop all the remaining cards from your right hand onto it, putting the marked card just above his card.

Cut the deck yourself and allow someone else to do so. Then, as you spread the cards on the table faces down, watch for the marked card. Run your finger back and forth over the face-down cards, and eventually stop on the card below the marked card.

Another way to find the card is to balance a table knife on your forefinger, and run it along the cards. When it reaches the chosen card, the knife dips downward as though the card was pulling it magnetically. Actually, you cause it to do this by turning your forefinger forward very slightly, disturbing the balance of the knife.

**MATERIALS**
Deck of playing cards
Single edge razor blade
(Handle carefully!)
Table knife

# THE VANISHING PRISONER

The performer shows a black jack and two red spot cards, mixes them a bit, and when the spectators try to pick out the jack it is found to have changed into a joker—and the missing jack has flown invisibly into the performer's pocket. Everything is done in the fairest possible manner and yet the spectators haven't the slightest clue as to what happened—a real baffler.

The performer asks a spectator, "*Would you like to join the FBI? Here's a test to find out if you would make a good detective. This black jack is Public Enemy No. 1. He is walking down the street with two friends when an FBI agent recognizes him.*" ①

"*The agent puts his hand on Jack's shoulder and says, 'You're under arrest. Come with me.'*" ②

The performer then removes the middle card and puts it face down on the table. ③ ④

"*The prisoner's friends decide to try to help Jack escape. They run after him. One goes to his right and starts an argument with the FBI agent. The other goes to his left.*" ⑤

"*Jack suddenly changes positions with his friend, Joe.*" ⑥

"*Then, before the FBI man can stop them, Lefty gets into the act and the two suspects on the outside change places. Now— which one would you put the handcuffs on? Which one is Jack?*" ⑦
Don't let the spectator pick up any of the cards. Tell him to point to one. It seems obvious that Jack must be on the left and most people select that card.

"*I'm glad you didn't choose either of these. You would have failed the test.*" ⑧

"*Good heavens! We all failed the test! Jack got away leaving some joker I never saw before in his place!*"

"*But the FBI finally caught Jack. They found him later hiding out—here.*" Bring out the duplicate jack from your shirt pocket. Put it on the table next to the joker and at the same time drop the two spot cards in your side pocket. ⑨

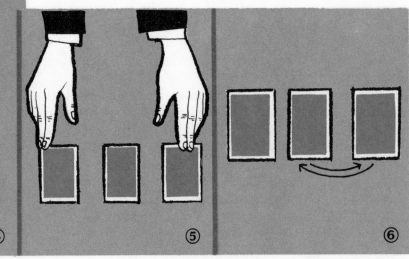

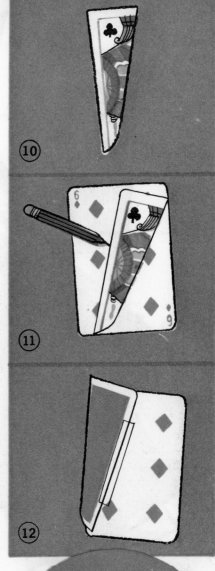

(10)   The jack of clubs shown at the beginning is really only half a jack. Cut a piece from an extra jack of clubs as shown.

(11)   Place this half card on one of the red cards in the position shown and make a pencil line along its left edge.

(12)   Turn the half card over to the left so that it is face down. Line its edge up with the pencil line, then fasten it in this position with Scotch® tape. Turn it face up again, the tape acting as a hinge, and your gimmick is complete.

Put the joker behind the hinged card, making sure that their top edges line up. Then put the other red card on both so that it hides the joker and the three cards will look as they do in picture No. 1. The real jack, of course, is in your pocket at the start.

Now simply follow the directions as shown in the pictures. Always take hold of the corner of what seems to be the jack, as in picture No. 2, while the cards still face the spectators. This is what makes it look so fair. If you turn the cards face down before doing this someone may think you switched the cards by sleight of hand. Do not make any quick moves at all; do everything slowly.

Note that after the middle card is removed from the fan (No. 3) the left hand moves the two red cards closer together so that the half card is covered as in picture No. 4.

Occasionally someone may try to cross you up by saying that the jack is the center card. You can't show this card by itself because you would expose the flap card. Simply pick up both spot cards, place one partly over the other and show them as in No. 8. Say, "*You're not watching carefully. These are Jack's friends.*" Then turn up the third card showing the joker.

If you have an extra card matching the one on which the flap is pasted in your pocket, you are prepared in case any really suspicious person, after examining the joker and the jack, asks to see the other cards. Simply bring out the two good spot cards, leaving the gimmicked one in the pocket.

**MATERIALS**
Deck of playing cards
Pencil
Scotch tape

## THE WITCH'S MESSAGE

The performer gives a spectator a sealed envelope. The spectator then shuffles the deck thoroughly, and deals and discards cards until he has only one left. In the envelope he finds a message which names this card.

This is an astonishing prediction because the performer never touches the cards except once for such a brief moment that the spectators forget about it.

PREPARATION: Take one card from the deck and make a scratch ①
mark about a quarter of an inch long on the card's edge at one end. Turn the card around and do the same at the other end. When this card is placed in the deck the scratch will show in a used deck as a narrow white line. If the deck is new, mark the ends of the card with a pencil instead of scratching them.

Write this message on a slip of paper: THE CARD YOU WILL BE ②
LOOKING AT WHEN YOU READ THIS IS THE EIGHT OF DIAMONDS. Of course, you use the name of the marked card. Seal this message in an envelope.

**MATERIALS**
Deck of playing cards
Envelope
Pencil
Piece of paper

Begin the trick by giving the cards to someone to shuffle. *"An extra good shuffle, please. We want to be absolutely sure the cards are well mixed."*

Then show the sealed envelope and give it to another spectator. *"I have a friend who is a witch and last week she gave me this message to give to you. But don't open it until I tell you."*

③ When the first spectator has finished shuffling take back the deck, glance at its end and look for the mark. If it is near the top or bottom cut the deck to bring it near the center. Say, *"I am going to cut the deck into two approximately equal halves."* Cut off all the cards above the marked card.

The easiest way to do this quickly is to open the deck slightly, two or three cards below the marked card, then let these few cards spring off the tip of your thumb and stop when you see the marked card fall.

Put the two halves down side by side in front of the spectator who shuffled. Then change your mind. *"No, I think it would be better if you cut the cards."* Pick up the half which was on the bottom, put it on the other packet, and square the cards. This leaves your marked card on top.

After the spectator cuts the deck into two halves, say, *"We need only one pile. Please touch either one."* You hope he will touch the pile which has the predicted card on top. If he does, say, *"Good. We'll discard the other pile."* If he touches the other pile, say, *"Good. We'll discard those."* Either way, this leaves the pile you want. *"Take the remaining pile, and deal one card to me and one to yourself, then another to me and another to yourself, and so on."*

④ Mentally count the cards as they are dealt. As soon as he has dealt seven cards into your pile, stop him. *"That's enough. Discard all the cards you have left."* Point to the pile he dealt to himself. *"And throw these out, too."*

Point to the pile he dealt to you. *"Now deal these again, the same way."* Watch to see that he gives you the first card on each deal. Again point to the cards he dealt to himself, tell him to discard them, and deal the remaining pile once more.

Again discard the dealer's pile. This leaves two cards, the one on the bottom being the predicted card. Move the top card to the right so they are side by side.

Again you offer him what seems to be a free choice, but isn't. *"There are two cards left. This time, instead of dealing, you may take either one."*

No matter which one he takes, say, *"Are you sure that's the one you want? Remember you could have taken the other. Do you want to change your mind?"* Sometimes he will, sometimes not. It makes no difference. When he finally decides definitely on one card, if he has chosen the prediction card, discard the other one, and say, *"Turn the card you chose face up."* If he chooses the other one, turn the prediction card face up saying, *"All right. That leaves this as the last card."*

Turn to the spectator who has the envelope. *"Now, open the envelope, and read aloud the message the witch wrote."*

① scratch shows as white line

② *The card you will be looking at when you read this is the Eight of diamonds*

③

④ discard deck — retain your 7 cards — discard his pile

## OBSERVATION TEST

The performer gives the spectators an observation test, which is so easy it seems impossible that anyone could fail yet everyone does. Two cards are placed in a hat. The performer removes one, shows it, and puts it in his pocket. When the spectators try to name the card left in the hat they fail, because the two cards have mysteriously changed places! This is repeated a second time.

PREPARATION: Take two quite different cards such as the ace of clubs and the king of hearts and paste them together, back to back. (Rubber cement is best.) Place this two-faced card in your trouser pocket with the king facing out.

PERFORMANCE: *"Many people are half asleep much of the time and they don't know it. I'm going to give you all a test to find out if you are really awake."*

Have someone examine a hat to make sure that it is empty, then place it brim up on your table. Remove from the deck the two ① cards that match your double-faced card. Hold one in each hand ② so that the audience sees their backs, then turn them faces out as you say, *"We will use two cards—a king and an ace."* Put both ③ cards into the hat face up and side by side.

Now explain what you are about to do. *"I am going to take one of the cards from the hat and put it in my pocket."* As you say this, ④ lift the king from the hat, its face toward the spectators, put it ⑤ in your pocket, and take hold of the double-faced card which is already there.

*"Then I will ask you to name the card which is left in the hat. If you are awake and watching that should be easy."* As you say this, bring the double-faced card with its king side showing from ⑥ your pocket and put it in the hat, king side up.

show backs
①

face up in hat
③

⑤

⑦

ace →

⑨

king
(double-
faced) →

show faces

②

④

double-faced king

⑥

⑧

ing

ace

⑩

ace

king

MATERIALS
Deck of playing cards
Rubber cement
Hat

*"Everybody ready? Let's go."* Reach into the hat, lift out the ace, show it without looking at it yourself, and pretend you are trying to confuse the spectators by misnaming it. *"I'll put the king in my pocket."* Before anyone can correct you, put the card in ⑦ your pocket and add, *"Now can you tell me the name of the card in the hat?"*

They think that you are trying to fool them in a very crude fashion and they object. They tell you that it was the ace you put in your pocket and that the king is still in the hat.

Shake your head. *"You're not watching. You aren't even listening."* Lift the double-faced card from the hat, turning it up so that ⑧ the ace side faces the audience. *"The ace is in the hat. I put the king in my pocket just as I said."* Exchange the cards in your pocket and bring out the king.

This impossible and unexpected result is your first climax. Now say, *"I'll give you a second chance. We'll do it again."* Put the double-faced card in the hat, ace side up, then put the king beside it.

Now lift the double-faced card from the hat, turning it so that ⑨ the king side is showing. This time name it correctly. *"I'll put the king in my pocket."* Put the card in your pocket and take hold of the ace which is already there. The spectators again reply that the ace is in the hat, and you show that they are wrong again by bringing the king from the hat and the ace from the pocket. ⑩

*"You're all sound asleep. I'm sorry but the whole class has to stay after school."*

Toss both cards to one side, faces down, so that the backs can be seen. Often a suspicious person will pick them up and examine them. He finds nothing wrong, of course, because the trick card that made this baffling double transposition possible is safely hidden in your pocket.

# How To Read Minds

### OUT-OF-THE-ROOM MINDREADING

There is a very old party stunt in which two persons claim to be able to read each other's thoughts. A leaves the room and the spectators select some object in the room. When A returns, B points to various objects one after another, asking, "Is this it?" A always knows when the correct object is touched.

This is really not very mystifying because everyone guesses that B is somehow signaling A and the problem is to figure out what system or code they are using. In one method the first time A returns, B touches a red object just before he touches the correct one; the second time he touches a white object, the third time a blue one.

This is merely a puzzle, not a real magic trick. The way to make it into a real baffler and fool everyone who knows the old methods is to hide the fact that an assistant is used. Arrange in secret ahead of time to have your brother or sister or a friend act as your secret assistant.

Gather together your ten different objects. Put them on a table or the floor in a circle. Tell the spectators that you can sometimes pick up thought waves the way a radio picks up radio waves. Ask them to choose one of the objects while you are out of the room.

**MATERIALS**
10 different objects:
Book
Pencil
Ashtray
Pen
Watch
Match folder, etc.

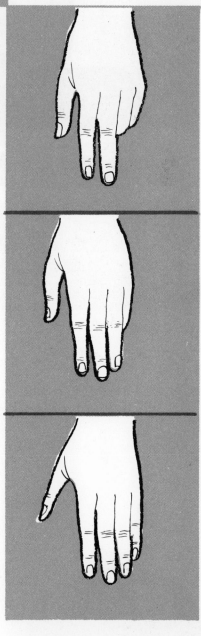

When you return stand where you can see your assistant's feet. Place your hand above various objects in turn, asking that the spectators all think "Stop!" when you reach the correct one. Your assistant signals you by moving one foot just a little, perhaps merely raising his toe slightly. But he does not do it when you touch the correct object because someone might notice it. He sends the signal as your hand is above the next object after the correct one. You continue to touch two or three more objects, then say, "*I think I went past it. You people aren't concentrating hard enough.*" Go back, touch one or two of the objects previously touched, then stop dramatically on the right one. This is no longer simply a puzzle; it looks like real mindreading.

A very dramatic and mystifying way to finish the trick is to come back into the room and immediately announce, "*I've got your thought already!*" Then name the correct object at once. This happens so quickly that it seems to rule out any form of signaling. And this time your assistant doesn't move at all.

You have agreed with him ahead of time that one of the objects is to be counted as No. 1. Or, it can be whichever object is first placed on the table. Your helper counts clockwise around the circle from this No. 1 object and indicates the position of the chosen one with a hand signal.

While you are still out of the room, he places his right hand on his knee with the proper number of fingers extended. If the fist is closed except for the thumb the chosen object is No. 1. If the forefinger is also extended it is No. 2. If thumb, forefinger, and middle finger are extended it is No. 3, and so on.

If the number is more than five he simply uses his left hand instead. You note the number of fingers extended and add five. A quick glance as you enter the room tells you all you need to know and you can name the correct object at once.

As a grand finale you can announce that you will try to name the correct object while you are still in the other room! When your helper hears this he knows it is his cue to be the person who selects the object to be thought about. And he touches any object which the two of you have agreed upon in advance.

This is a real mystery and you will fool the adults in your audience, especially those who know the old methods.

## DO-IT-YOURSELF MINDREADING

"*Reading minds*," the magician says, "*is really quite easy. Anyone can do it.*" He takes a volunteer from the audience who admits that he or she can't read minds but would like to learn how. This person surprises everyone by finding several chosen cards which have been buried in the deck.

You do not need to arrange anything with this person in advance. You can do it with anyone and they will be willing to agree quite honestly that nothing has been prearranged. The secret here is that you enlist this person as an assistant *after* the trick begins. Your only preparation is to print or type, so that it is easy to read, the following instructions on a piece of paper somewhat smaller than a playing card.

INSTRUCTIONS
REMOVE THE CARDS IN
THE DECK WHICH FACE
THE WRONG WAY. GIVE
THEM TO ME ONE AT A
TIME. THEN HIDE THIS
CARD BEHIND THE
OTHERS.

Paste this paper on the face of the joker, or on any extra card from another deck which has the same back design as the deck you are using. Then put this card face down on top of your face-down deck.

Begin by saying that anyone can read minds and then select a spectator who would like to be able to do it. Seat him in a chair at one end of the room with his back to the audience. You can also pretend to put him in a hypnotic trance.

Bring out your deck of cards and riffle shuffle it, keeping the instruction card in place on the top of the deck (page 53). Spread the deck and have three people each take out a card. Tell the choosers not to look at their cards until you have turned your back because you want everyone to be convinced that you do not know what they are.

Actually, you turn your back for another reason. You have a secret move to perform. Take the face-down instruction card from the top of the pack and turn all the other cards face up under it. Now, if you keep the deck neatly squared you seem to be holding a face-down deck.

Face the audience again and go to the person who took the first card. Take it from him and push it face down into the deck somewhere in the lower half. Keep the deck squared as you do this so none of the face-up cards will show. If you use cards which have white margins around the back design you will have no trouble.

Push the second chosen card into the deck above the first one near the middle, and place the third card into the upper half of the deck. Then say, *"This is an extremely difficult test for a beginner. He has only three chances in fifty-two of finding even one card—unless he can read your thought waves. Everyone please concentrate."* Turn to the amateur mentalist. *"Will you agree that you have seen none of the chosen cards and haven't the slightest idea what any of them are?"* He has to say "Yes" to this because he is still completely in the dark.

Now you make a second secret move. Go to the seated volunteer and reach around him to hand him the deck. When the deck is hidden from the others by his body push the top card over to one side with your thumb. Turn your hand over and drop the instruction card face up in his lap. Then give him the deck.

He will see the instructions and read them while you continue talking. Go to the person who took the first card and say, "*Our master mentalist will attempt to read your mind first. Please concentrate as hard as you can—and send your thought waves in his direction. You know how to do that, don't you?*" If he says he doesn't, tell him to try anyway.

Return to the volunteer and tell him, "*Run through the deck and when you come to the card that is being thought of take it out and give it to me.*"

The first face-down card he comes to will be the first chosen card. When he removes it, reach down, take it from him, and hold it up, back toward the audience. Ask the first person to name his card aloud, then show the card you hold. "*That's wonderful!*" you say. "*Do you think you can do it again?*"

Ask the second person to concentrate on the card he chose. When the mental wizard, who by now is having lots of fun helping out because he is getting all the applause, finds the next face-down card, show that he has succeeded again. Then repeat with the final card.

Finish by taking the deck from him and ask him to stand up and take a bow. Tell him that it is the most remarkable first attempt at mindreading you have ever seen and that perhaps he should go into the business professionally. Then add, "*But if I were you I wouldn't teach any of these other people how to do it because we would have too much competition. Thank you very much for your kind assistance.*"

Put the deck in your pocket. Later, if you use the deck again, simply take it out, leaving the instruction card behind.

## THE GREAT BOOK TEST

This is as mystifying a mental stunt as you can do. You use an assistant whom you say has X-ray vision and can see through walls! If you do this at a party have him wear a turban made from a turkish towel. Since this looks funny the audience will think you are going to do a joke stunt of some sort, and they will be completely amazed when it turns out to look like the real thing.

Send your mentalist into another room and see that the door is closed. You can even send him into a room upstairs. Show the audience a book and announce that it has 315 pages (or whatever the number is). Point out that there are about thirty lines on each page and about ten words in each line. Ask anyone to call out a page number. Then someone else calls a number between one and thirty, and a third person a number between one and ten.

Give the book to someone and have him turn to the page called, then count down to the line whose number was called, and count across to the word that falls on the third number. Have him show this word to everyone and caution them that it is not to be said aloud. Then tell the spectator who has the book to close it, take it into the other room, and give it to the Man Who Can See Through Walls, and return.

*"There are many thousands of words in that book,"* you say, *"but our Hindu mystic, Johnny Jones* (or whatever his name is), *will attempt to find the very word you chose! He is the only man in the world who can perform this amazing feat! He has been practicing it for ten hours a day for forty years."* If Johnny is only ten this will get a laugh and they will still expect a joke of some sort.

But then, a moment later, Johnny returns with a folded slip of paper. When you ask him if he succeeded, he says, *"Yes. It was easy."* Now ask everyone to name the chosen word aloud, then tell someone to take the paper Johnny has, open it, and read aloud what is written on it. It is the chosen word! Johnny takes a bow.

This miracle requires a little preparation. You and Johnny must each have a pencil and a slip of paper. And the book you use is prepared. Remove the paper dust jacket. Put a sheet of paper on the cover of the book and a sheet of carbon paper over it. Scotch® tape them in position as shown. Then replace the jacket.

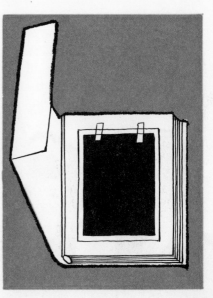

Since several numbers are selected, it is only natural that you should make a note of them. When you ask for the page number, take out your slip of paper and pencil. Put the paper on the book and write down the number. Also write down the other numbers, one under another. Since your paper is over the carbon the numbers will be secretly transferred to the paper hidden under the book jacket.

All Johnny has to do when he gets the book, is turn back the jacket, note the numbers, look up the word, and write it down. Then he removes the carbon paper and the concealed message paper and hides them.

# THE PSYCHIC DETECTIVE

The performer solves a murder mystery by mindreading. This is one of the most dramatic and mystifying party tricks you can do.

*"We are,"* you announce, *"going to play a game of murder and I will demonstrate a remarkable new method of crime detection that will revolutionize police procedure and put all criminals out of business. I am a psychic detective and I am going to solve a baffling murder case faster than Sherlock Holmes ever did. The scene of the crime is here in this room. While I am at headquarters in the next room with the door closed, you people select someone to be the victim and someone else to play the part of the murderer. Then call headquarters and I'll come back and try to solve the case in which the murderer hasn't left a single clue!"*

When this has been done you return and say, *"I am going to question the witnesses to the crime and you must play fair and give truthful answers, but don't say a word out loud. Just think the answers. I solve all my cases the hard way. I'll try to find the victim first."*

Go to someone, put your hand on his forehead, close your eyes and say, *"First question. Is the victim in this room? Don't answer out loud. Just think one word, either 'Yes' or 'No.' Good! You concentrate very well. You are thinking 'Yes.' Now answer this question the same way. Is the victim on this side of the room? You're thinking . . . concentrate a little harder, please. . . . That's better . . . you are thinking 'No.' "*

Turn to someone else. *"Now you tell me—just by thinking—is the victim a boy or girl?"* Pause briefly after each question and pretend to concentrate. Make it look as though reading minds is hard work. *"Something's wrong. I'm getting a lot of static! Either you don't think very well, or . . . Oh, I see . . . it's coming from that direction."* Point to someone else. *"From you. Will you please stop thinking altogether. I never heard such a racket."* Ask the question again. *"That's better. It's coming in very faintly, but I get it. You are thinking: 'Boy.' "*

Don't bother to ask if this is correct. Since everyone knows the answer they can see that you are scoring 100%. What they don't know is that you spotted the victim as soon as you came into the room and that you know all the answers before you ask the questions. How? We'll get to that in a moment.

Next, go to a third person and say, *"I'm going to name all the boys on this side of the room. Think 'No' if the name is wrong and 'Yes' when I name the victim."* Even better, ask this question of the victim himself. *"Bob? . . . You're thinking: 'No.' George? Still 'No.' Harry?"* Pause a moment, then scowl. *"It's not coming in. Does thinking just a couple of words tire you out like that? Try again, please. That's better—but you're still thinking 'No' and that can't be right. I've named all the boys . . . oh, I see. I forgot you! Think 'Yes' or 'No.' Now, are you the victim? You're thinking: 'Yes'! Thank you!"*

*"Now let's see if we can get a confession from the murderer."* Do this in the same way, asking questions of several people. Play it straight part of the time, building up the mystery by seriously pretending that you are really reading minds. But now and then make it funny. Perhaps when you ask, *"Is the murderer a boy or girl?"* you concentrate a moment and then look at the person who is thinking the answer and say, *"You're thinking 'Boy' . . . but I don't like the way you think it. You're trying to cross me up. You're lying. It's really a girl. Isn't that right? Think 'Yes' or 'No.' Aha! So you admit it. I've a good notion to arrest you for perjury."*

When you are questioning a girl, pretend to have trouble getting her thoughts. Like this: *"You seem to be tuned to a different wave length. Let me hold your hand. That often helps."* Pause a moment. *"It's still pretty faint. I may have to hold your hand quite a while."* Look at the others. *"This is the part of the detective business I like best."* Then ask the girl: *"I hope you don't mind? No. That's a leading question and you might incriminate yourself. You'd better not answer."*

If there is an adult in the group, you can have some fun by pretending that his mind is very difficult to read. *"Your thought waves are terribly confused, did you know that? Everything is all mixed up."*

A good dramatic way to unmask the murderer at the end is to ask the victim to stand, take his or her hand, and say, *"We're going to catch the murderer now. You follow me. If I walk in the right direction you think 'Yes.' If I go in the wrong direction you think 'No.'"* Move off in the wrong direction at first, then change your course several times as if receiving the mental directions, finally stop before the murderer and say dramatically: *"The case is solved! You're under arrest!"*

The secret is so simple that your advance preparation can be done in a moment or two. Tell someone that you need a secret assistant and that if he will help you and keep it a secret he will learn how to read minds so he can do it himself. All he has to do as soon as the victim has been selected is to sit or stand in exactly the same position as the victim. When you return to the room, a quick glance at your assistant and a look around at the others tells you all you need to know to answer your first questions. Then, after you find the victim, your assistant changes his position to match that of the murderer. This is not only one of the easiest and most mystifying tricks you can do but also one of the most amusing. You can have loads of fun with it.

# THE HELPFUL GHOST

A blank slip of paper, a lead pencil point, and a card chosen by a spectator are covered with a handkerchief. The performer blows a whistle summoning the spirits and when the paper is opened it is found to bear a message naming the card.

PREPARATION: You need a pad of paper slightly larger than a playing card. On one sheet, in shaky handwriting, write *This is the six of clubs*, and sign the message: *George.* Break the point off a lead pencil, place it in the center of the paper and then crumple it, message inside, into a small ball. Put this and a whistle in a right-hand pocket. Put the six of clubs face down underneath the pad of paper and carry them in another pocket. You also need a clean, folded handkerchief.

PERFORMANCE: Begin by announcing, *"I once lived in a haunted house, and became very good friends with a ghost named George. I am going to ask him to do a trick for you."* Ask someone to shuffle the cards. While this is being done get the pad of paper and card. Hold the pad with the card concealed under it in your right hand, then take the deck back with your left.

Lay the pad on the deck just long enough to tear off the top sheet and give it to someone to examine. Then put the pad aside, leaving the six of clubs on the deck.

Put the deck down before a spectator and ask him to cut it into ① two halves. Pick up the bottom half and place it crosswise on the top half saying, *"This will mark the cut."*

Bring out a pencil, break off its point, put it on the paper and crumple the paper into a ball. Place it on the table and get your handkerchief. Shake it out as you say, *"Since George is a ghost he will only work in the dark."* Spread the handkerchief out over the paper ball.

Now say, *"We'll also put the card to which you cut under the handkerchief."* Lift off the upper half of the deck, remove the top ② card of the lower half and slide it under the handkerchief. (This is not the card to which the spectator cut. It was the top card of the deck, but the spectators will, by now, have forgotten just how the deck was cut; you have given them too many other things to watch.)

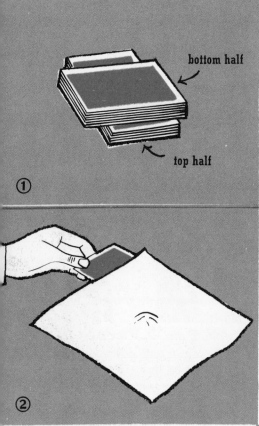

① 

bottom half

top half

② 

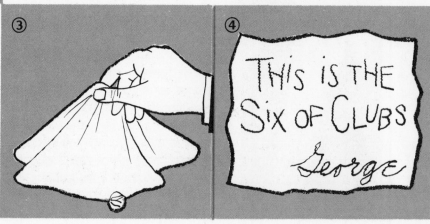

③ 

④ 

THIS IS THE SIX OF CLUBS

*George*

MATERIALS
Pad of paper
Lead pencil
Deck of playing cards
Whistle
Handkerchief

Put your right hand in your pocket, place the paper ball which contains the message on the second, third, and fourth fingers and close them around it. Take the whistle between thumb and forefinger and bring it out.

"*This,*" you say, "*is a spirit whistle and George always comes when I blow it.*" Take it in your left hand, put it to your mouth, and blow. "*George,*" you add, "*is a very fast worker. He comes and goes so quickly you probably didn't even see him.*"

③ Reach for the center of the handkerchief and grasp the ball under it through the cloth. As you lift handkerchief and ball upward, open your fingers and allow the hidden ball to fall behind the handkerchief.

④ Ask a spectator to unfold the paper, and as he does so, put the handkerchief in your pocket. Have the ghost message read aloud and then tell someone to turn the chosen card face up. George has named it!

Another way to get the card on top after the deck has been shuffled is to mark it on the edge (as explained in "The Electric Card," page 74). Instead of hiding it under the pad, leave it in the deck and then, after the shuffle, simply cut it to the top, and riffle shuffle the deck once yourself, leaving the card on top.

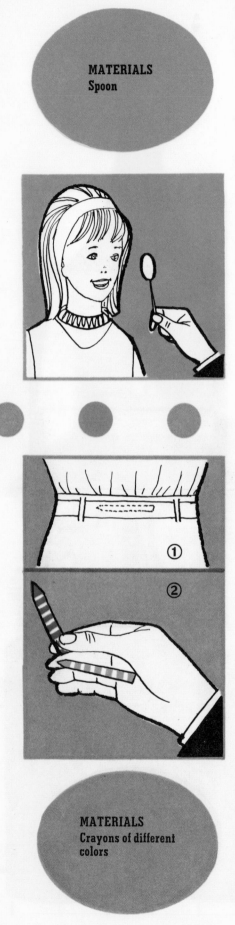

**MATERIALS**
Spoon

**MATERIALS**
Crayons of different colors

## GHOST PHOTOS

Show your audience a spoon and say, *"This is a new camera I have invented which takes magic ghost pictures. Anyone can take good photos with it without any complicated instructions."*

Select someone to act as the photographer and give him the spoon. *"All you have to do is hold this in front of someone's face while you count to five. It needs a five-second exposure."* Then leave the room until this has been done. When you return, look into the spoon and announce the name of the person whose ghost photo you pretend you can see there.

The secret here is the same undercover helper using the same hand signals as in "Out-of-the-Room Mindreading." He counts himself as No. 1, then counts to his left around the room and signals the number of the person whose picture was taken. The spectators will be so interested in examining the spoon for some gimmick that isn't there, that they will never suspect the real method.

You can repeat this several times and at the end you can say, *"I could make a million dollars if I put this camera on the market except for one thing. I'm the only person who can see the photos."*

## COLOR DIVINATION

You have prepared for this trick earlier by hiding one crayon ① whose color you know under your belt in back.

This time you ask the spectator to mix the crayons and then give them all to you. Face the audience again, reach under your belt, obtain the hidden crayon and hold it between thumb and forefinger. Put a second crayon in the right hand, holding it be- ② tween the end of the third finger and the palm of the hand.

Now name the crayon whose color you know. Bring the right hand to the front and show the crayon, being careful to hold your hand with its back toward the spectators so they cannot see the second crayon in the palm of the hand. Glance at the hidden crayon and note its color as you put the first crayon aside.

Put your hand behind your back again, take the second crayon between thumb and forefinger and put a third one in the palm of the hand. Name the color of the crayon you just glimpsed. Bring it out, show it, and get a look at the third crayon.

Continue until you have named the colors of all the crayons. This is most effective when done quickly because the faster you do it the more impossible it seems.

## SUPER TOUCH

Here you not only read colors with your fingertips but also identify playing cards while they are behind your back. Prepare for this by taking the four aces from the deck and three other cards which you arrange behind the aces in an order which you can memorize.

These are good cards to use. It is easy to remember 3, 6, 9 because you merely add three to each card to get the next one. Notice that the suits are arranged so that the initial letters of *C*lubs, *H*earts, *S*pades, and *D*iamonds are in the same order as they appear in the word *CHaSeD*. This arrangement makes it easy to memorize all the cards in order.

① Square this packet of cards and attach them with a paper clip to the back of your belt under your coat.

Begin the trick by giving someone the remainder of the deck to shuffle. *"I'll turn my back,"* you say, *"so that I can't possibly see any of the cards."* After the cards have been shuffled ask that they be handed to you behind your back. Then face the spectators.

*"I will try to read the names of the cards merely by feeling their faces."* As you say this pull the hidden packet of cards from the paper clip and place them on the deck. Close your eyes, pretend to concentrate, and then say, *"The top card feels like the three of clubs."* Bring it to the front, show it, and discard it. Concentrate again. *"The next card is the six of dia— No. It's red but it feels more like a heart. The six of hearts."*

It is always effective when doing mental tricks to pretend to make a mistake occasionally, then correct it.

After you have named the third card, announce that you will now try something far more difficult. *"I will run through the deck and try to find an ace."* Count off several cards so that the counting can be heard but without disarranging their order. Say, *"That feels like an ace—I think it's the ace of clubs."* Put the counted-off cards back on the deck and bring the top card to the front, showing that you have named it correctly. Find the other three the same way, pretending each time to hunt through the deck.

Sometimes a spectator may suspect that the aces have been marked in some way so that they do feel different, and he will examine the cards and perhaps the rest of the deck without, of course, finding any difference.

② If you want to do this when you are not wearing a coat, slip the packet of cards inside your trousers. Your belt will hide the paper clip.

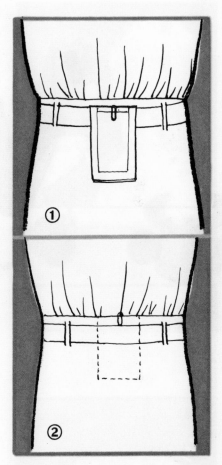

**MATERIALS**
Deck of playing cards
Paper clip

# Miscellaneous Magic

## CUTTING A BOY INTO THREE PIECES

The performer borrows a boy from the audience, grasps his shirt at the neck, pulls it quickly, and the shirt passes right through the boy and comes off! This unexpected surprise always gets a big laugh and a big hand. This is a perfect party trick.

The borrowed boy isn't as innocent as he looks. In fact, you have a little session in private with him before the show, during which you make a few preparations. Have him remove his coat or sweater, then his shirt.

① Lay the shirt over his back as shown here, then button his shirt cuffs around his wrists.

② Put the collar around his neck and button it in place. Draw up enough of the shirt over his shoulders so that you can button two more buttons. Then hold his coat so that he can get back into it again. If he is wearing a tie put that back on, too.

③ With his coat on and buttoned he looks as though he were properly dressed although he actually isn't in the shirt at all. He rejoins the rest of the party.

**MATERIALS**
Boy wearing coat, tie, and regular shirt

①

②

③

④

When you are ready to perform the trick announce, *"In this next miracle, one of the most dangerous feats of all magic, I intend to cut a boy into three parts! Will someone volunteer?"*

Usually, if you ask for volunteers, everybody wants to get into the act, but this hint of danger may prevent that. If anyone does offer to assist before your assistant can do so, you merely rule him out because he's too fat or too skinny. Your prepared assistant is chosen because he looks just right and you bring him forward and seat him on a chair.

Turn to the audience and ask, *"Now, does anyone have a cross-cut saw?"*

At this, your assistant gets up and starts back for his seat pretending that he has changed his mind about helping.

Grab him. *"You sit down and stay there. Apparently nobody brought a saw today so I'll have to cut you in three pieces the painless way. I promise it won't hurt—much."* As you say that he tries to get up again but you hold him down.

Then pull out one of his cuffs and unbutton it. Do the same with the other. Remove his tie and unbutton the shirt buttons at the top. *"I'm doing this,"* you explain, *"so you can breathe easier and won't faint."*

Stand behind the seated assistant and grasp the back of his shirt collar. *"Watch! At the count of three I am going to pull his shirt right up through his arms, cutting them both off! Ready! One!"*

Here your assistant can say, "Excuse me. I've just remembered I have to leave."

*"Quiet!"* you tell him. *"Two! . . . Three!"*

④ Pull the shirt straight up fast so that it comes clear out of his jacket.

*"What do you know about that?"* you say. *"The shirt went right through him!"* Thank your assistant and, as he leaves, add, *"If your arms should fall off later, let me know. I have some tape."*

① ② ③

## MAGIC RESTORATION

The magician tears a dollar bill (use play money) in half, folds the torn pieces into a small packet and blows on it. When he opens it the money has multiplied. He now has two new undamaged bills.

Get a package of play money at your toy or stationery store. ①
Put two bills together and fold them in half, then in half again, ②
then once in the other direction, making a packet a little over an ④
inch square.

Take a third bill and fold it in the same way. Put this folded bill underneath the packet of two bills. Lay both packets on five or six unfolded bills and clip them together with a paper clip as ⑤
shown here.

Fold the package of bills in half and put them in your pocket. When you begin the trick, take out the bills and open them, keeping the small folded packets on the side away from the audience so they cannot be seen. Separate the bill nearest you from the others and pull it, together with the small packets, out from under ⑥
the paper clip.

Now tear the bill into two pieces as you say, "*When I went to* ⑦
*the store for my mother the other day I tried to pay the store keeper fifty cents by giving him half of a dollar bill.*" Put the half in your left hand behind the other half.

Now fold the two halves into a packet the same size as the hidden bills. "*He wouldn't take it and I don't understand why.*" Take the bills between thumb and fingers of the left hand and place them on the two middle fingers of the right hand. Hold them in ⑧
place with the right thumb.

Bring the right hand up to the mouth and blow on the bills. Say, "*All you have to do is blow like this on a torn bill . . .*"

Push forward with your thumb, sliding the top packet to the fingertips. Then unfold it and show that you have two new bills. ⑨

"*. . . and each half dollar becomes a whole dollar!*"

⑤

⑥

⑦

⑧ ⑨

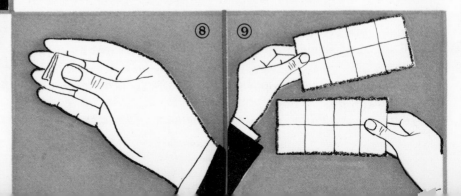

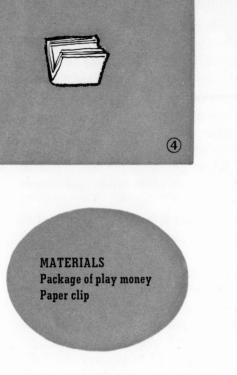

④

At this point some spectators will suspect that you have exchanged the torn pieces for new bills by sleight of hand—but now comes the magic. Take both bills in your right hand and lower your right hand to your side. Push off the next folded packet and let it fall to the floor. Don't look at it; you want everyone to think this was accidental.

Now take the two bills into your right hand and put them away in your pocket, leaving the torn pieces there, too. Your audience will be watching the packet you dropped and will think they have the trick all figured out. Then you notice it yourself, pick it up, and say: *"Oh well, mistakes can happen to anybody. Of course, magicians never worry about little things like that."*

Blow on the packet and then unfold it, showing that what everyone thought were the torn pieces are all one piece again—a perfectly restored bill!

You can have a lot of fun with this trick because the audience will enjoy the joke as much as you do. Practice it several times before you perform it so that you can do it smoothly, and memorize the patter so that you do not have to hesitate and think what you are going to say next.

## THE MESSAGE FROM THE ASHES

The names of several spectators are written down, each one on a separate slip of paper. A spectator chooses one paper at random and the others are burned. When the magician rubs the ashes on his forearm a name appears there magically. It proves to be the one that was chosen!

① You prepare for this by writing the first name of one of the people who will be in your audience on your arm with soap. Cut a narrow piece of soap from the end of a bar, dip it in water, and write. Even better, make a strong soap solution and apply it with a water color brush. When dry the writing is invisible.

Begin by asking various people to call out their names. When the first name is called write it on a small pad of paper, tear the sheet off, fold it, and drop it into a hat. Do the same with the other names. Five or six names are enough.

Ask someone to close his eyes, reach into the hat, mix the papers, and then take out one. Put the remaining slips in an ash tray and burn them. Roll up your sleeve and rub some of the ashes briskly across your arm. The invisible letters you put there earlier

② will suddenly turn black. Ask the person who has the chosen paper to open it and read the selected name aloud. He finds that it is the same!

This happens because when you wrote down the names you wrote the same name on all the papers no matter what was called. Burning the papers, of course, destroys the evidence of your trickery. The sudden appearance of the chosen name is very baffling and mysterious.

# THE

# LIE

# DETECTOR II

Tell your audience that you are going to demonstrate a new kind of lie detector which you have invented. Ask someone to play the part of a bank robber. *"You had a list of the names of the other members of the gang and you tried to tear it up when we arrested you, but we managed to get the pieces."*

As you say this tear a piece of paper into smaller pieces and give one of them to the bank robber with a pencil. *"Write down the name of the leader of the gang on this paper without letting me see it. Just his first name."* When he has done this give him several more pieces of paper. *"Now, write some other first names on these pieces—any names at all."*

Turn your back so you cannot see what is written. When he has finished give him a hat. *"Put all the papers into this hat and stir them up so they are thoroughly mixed, then let me have it."*

Now show a spoon and announce that this is your new simplified lie detector. You can use anything—a table knife, a match folder, a bunch of keys. *"The first name you wrote was the name of the leader of the gang. I am going to find it by asking you some questions and you are to answer 'No' to all of them."*

Hold the lie detector a few inches in front of his mouth. Take a piece of paper from the hat, and ask, *"Is your leader's name George?"* reading whatever name is on the paper. After the spectator says "No," examine the spoon as if it held some clue. Do this with a second paper, and a third, and so on.

When you come to the correct paper you tell the spectator that he is lying.

Your audience will be so busy examining the spoon and trying to figure out how your lie detector works that they will never spot the real secret. Your clue is in the torn papers.

At the beginning you fold a sheet of paper into thirds, turn it sideways and fold into thirds again, creasing the folds each time. Then open the paper out and tear along the creases.

As you tear the paper always keep the center square nearest you so that it is on top of the other pieces when you finish. This is the piece you pass out first.

After the papers have been mixed you can always recognize this one because it is the only one with *four* torn edges. All the others have one or two straight edges. It isn't necessary to have names written on all the other papers; five or six will do. Just be sure that the important name is on the piece with four torn edges.

**MATERIALS**
Paper
Pencil
Hat
Spoon

The magician breaks an egg into a borrowed hat, adds flour, stirs the mixture, says the magic word, and produces several cupcakes from the hat. The perfect trick for a birthday party.

You will need the following props:

1. Two or three cup cakes. If they are frosted, get the kind that have a hard frosting.

2. A paper napkin.

3. A two- or three-pound paper flour sack.

4. An opaque plastic drinking glass.

5. A blown egg. You make this by puncturing a hole in one end of a fresh egg with a needle or pin. Enlarge the hole until it is about one eighth of an inch in diameter by chipping the edges. Make another hole in the other end of the egg. Hold the egg over a dish and blow into it until all the contents have come out. Do this well in advance of your show so the egg will have time to dry out. It is a good idea to prepare two or three eggs at once so that you do not need to fix another each time you do the trick.

6. A faked tablespoon. Not one of mother's silver spoons; get a cheap one from the dime store. Put two tablespoons of plaster of Paris in a cup and add water a little at a time, stirring it until you have a heavy, thick mixture. Very little water is needed. Put the plaster into your tablespoon, piling it up in the center so that it is a heaping spoonful. After the plaster has set slide it out of the spoon. Coat the bowl of the spoon with a good glue or airplane cement and replace the plaster. When dry, look at the spoon from the bottom and if any of the plaster projects over the edge of the spoon trim it off with a knife.

Put a pinch or two of flour into the flour sack together with the cup cakes. Put the faked tablespoon and the blown egg into an opaque plastic glass. Arrange these articles on a tray so that you can obtain them all at once when you are ready to do the trick.

Begin the trick by borrowing a hat. Make sure beforehand that someone in your audience has one. If not, give somebody one before the show so that you can pretend to borrow it. The trick is much funnier if the audience thinks you are using a borrowed hat.

**MATERIALS**
Egg
Flour
Paper napkin
Opaque plastic
drinking glass
Needle or pin
Dish
2 or 3 pound flour sacks
Inexpensive tablespoon
Plaster of Paris
Cup
Water
Glue or airplane cement
Knife
Tray
Wand

Show the inside of the hat so that it can be seen that there is nothing in it. Then place it upside down on your table. "*I need the hat,*" you say, "*because I am going to do some baking and I forgot to bring a mixing bowl.*" As you say this, pick up the egg and crack it on the edge of the glass.

Hold the egg over the hat and, just as you break the two halves ① apart, lower the egg down into the hat so that no one can see that there was nothing in it. Put the egg shells aside and wipe your fingers with the paper napkin. Pretending that you got egg on them is a bit of acting that helps convince the spectators that the egg is real.

Now take the spoon from the glass, holding it with its bottom toward the audience. Dip it into the flour sack, turn it so that it is level, and bring out what appears to be a heaping spoonful of ② flour. Put this into the hat and again turn the spoon sideways. Bring it out and go immediately to the sack for more flour. Do this three times, then stir the egg and flour that is supposed to be in the hat.

"*This,*" you say, looking into the hat, "*is a real messy-looking mess. That's why I never use my own hat.*" Then add, "*We need more flour.*"

Put the spoon back in the glass. Pick up the flour sack and dump its contents into the hat. Keep the mouth of the sack down inside the hat when you do this so the audience can't see what comes out. Then shake the sack as you lift it up, causing the pinch of flour it contains to dust out. This will convince everyone that you are really using flour.

Look at the person from whom you borrowed the hat and say, "*I do hope this works. It is the first time I've tried it.*" This always gets a good laugh; everybody is glad it isn't their hat. Now you can wave a wand over the hat, shoot a cap pistol at it, or simply say a few magic words, then step forward and pass out the cakes. If it is a birthday party make sure the birthday boy or girl gets the first one. As you take out the last cake hold the hat so that the inside can be seen, then return it to the owner, and thank him for the use of his mixing bowl.

# INK TO WATER

A glass of ink is transformed into a glass of water which the performer drinks.

PREPARATION: Make a cylinder of black cloth which will just fit ①
the inside of the glass you use. It should extend from the bottom
up to within about an inch of the top. Sew one end of a length of
fine black silk thread to the upper edge of the cloth at the seam,
and tie a small cork to the opposite end. When the cloth is in the
glass the cork should hang down behind the glass on the outside ②
a little below the upper edge of the cloth.

Put enough water in the glass so that it just reaches the upper
edge of the cloth, and press the cloth against the sides of the
glass. At a little distance it gives the appearance of ink.

You also need a strip of thin wood (use a tongue depressor) ③
about half an inch wide and five or six inches long. Cover one end
of this on one side only with the ink, the inked part being as long
as the depth of the "ink" in your glass.

Ink a second stick in the same way and then, while the ink is
still wet, wipe it on a cleansing tissue so that it leaves a smear on
the paper. Refold the tissue and have it on your table, ink side
down.

PERFORMANCE: *"This glass holds a half pint of ink which I no
longer need because I just bought a ball-point pen. I'll do a trick
with it."*

Pick up the stick, holding it with the uninked side toward the
spectators. Put it in the water and as you stir, turn it so that the ④
inked side shows when you take it out. ⑤

Pick up the cleansing tissue and wipe the stick off with it. Hold ⑥
the tissue so that the ink smear can be seen, then wrap the stick
in it and put it aside. Your pretense that you are being careful not
to get ink on anything, the changed appearance of the stick, and
the ink smear all supply "proof" that the glass does hold ink.

Cover the glass with a handkerchief. Then fire a cap pistol at
it or blow your magic whistle. Grasp the cork through the hand- ⑦
kerchief and lift the handkerchief up. This pulls the cloth from
the glass, and the ink has changed to water.

**MATERIALS**
Glass
Black cloth
Fine black silk thread
Small cork
Water
Tongue depressor
Ink
Cleansing tissue
Handkerchief
Cap pistol or whistle
Candy bonbons

"Some people," you say, "think that this trick is done using a mixture of hydrochloric acid and arsenic. I'll prove that isn't so. Here. You drink it." Offer it to a spectator. He probably doesn't trust you at all by now and will refuse. Those spectators who know some chemistry will suspect that chemicals were used and you give them a final shock by drinking it yourself.

You can also change the ink to candy. Fill the glass with water first to dampen the cloth, then pour it out. Put several candy bonbons in the glass, stacking them up in the center so that they won't interfere with the stirring you do later. After you cover the glass, shake it a bit so that the stack of candy falls in a heap. After the ink is changed to candy, eat one yourself to prove it is edible, then pass the others out. Any trick in which your audience gets free candy is sure to be a success!

## THE

## GREAT

## PAPER BAG

## MYSTERY

Houdini was a magician who became world famous by specializing in escapes. He freed himself of complicated rope ties, handcuffs, leg irons, and straitjackets. He escaped from jails, from milk cans filled with water, and from boxes into which he was nailed and then dropped into the river. One of his most baffling and mysterious escapes was from a large paper sack. Unlike many of his feats which were difficult and often dangerous, this one is easy but looks completely impossible. It is a party stunt which will amaze all your friends.

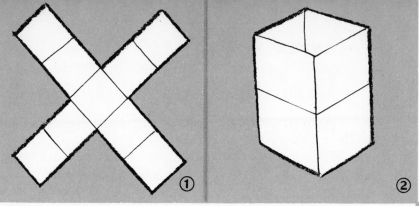
① ②

PREPARATION: You need a large paper bag, big enough to get into. Stationers sell brown wrapping paper in sheets, about 30″ x 40″. You will need nine of these, one for the bottom of the bag and two for each of the sides. Examine a paper grocery bag. Note how it is folded, and fold your bag in the same way so that it can be carried easily.

Use one of the white glues and paste the sheets together to form a bag, as shown. You also need a pair of shoelaces and a sharp pocket knife.

PERFORMANCE: Show the bag and a shoe lace to the spectators and let them examine both. Announce that you are going to let them tie you into the bag. *"Anyone,"* you say, *"can escape from a paper bag by tearing his way out, but I am going to disappear completely while in the bag and then magically reappear outside— leaving the bag unharmed!"* Take your audience into a room which has a door that can be closed. Give someone a shoelace, then crawl into the bag, feet first. Tell them to close the mouth of the bag and tie it securely with the shoelace. After this is done, they are to leave the room, and close the door. You should have one friend in the crowd who makes sure that they do this and don't pretend to leave and stay to watch you get out.

After they have gone, push the blade of your knife through the paper as close to the shoelace as possible. Cut the lace, open the bag, and come out.

Retie the bag with the second shoelace so that it covers the small slit you made in the paper. Examine the cut lace to see how many knots were tied in it so that you can retie the bag in about the same way. Then hide your knife and the cut shoelace. Open the door, rejoin the others, and give them the bag to examine.

Later cut the shoelace off and trim five or six inches from the end of the bag. This gets rid of the slit and the bag is ready to use again. You can do the trick several times before having to make another bag.

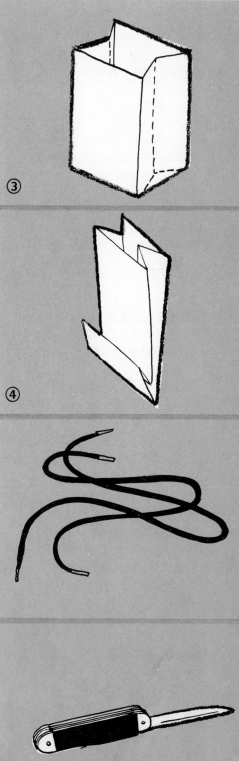
③
④

**MATERIALS**
Brown wrapping paper
Grocery bag
White glue
Pair of shoelaces
Pocket knife
(Handle carefully!)